What People Are

Your Soul,

Marzcia speaks straight to our Soul. No doubt. We received her message. She gives us the pathway to go in a safe way to find the Light and the pillar of it, and reinforces us to go in our path with more confidence. She gives us advice that there are some blocks, but it gives us a certainty that we have help from our lineage to heal ourselves. This book is to be read not only once. It is a guide for our life in this world. She is a truth healer.

In my life, I have never experienced someone like Marzcia. Her book must be spread all over to bring some comfort and understanding for those who need some confirmation of our soul pathway. She speaks straight to our soul. Be ready for it.
Sonia Gomes, PhD, Clínical Psychologist, SE Senior Faculty, and Founder of SOMA-Embodiment-Touch & Movement Trauma Therapy

Marzcia's book contains the loving answers and explanations that people of today need in order to understand themselves and to loosen what is stuck inside. It gives the needed help for the soul to live freely and happily in a peaceful body so that the experience of living life with joy and purpose can be fully expressed. With fine and gentle calls for self-reflection and exercises, everyone is helped in an understandable way.

Marzcia truly belongs to the amazing Universal Tribe of living, incomprehensibly loving, gentle and powerful spiritual healers who act as absolutely necessary birth attendants for people on Earth today.
Marianne Camille Tiffanie Kirkskov, MD, Healer & Author Healer & Author | Bridge Of Stars Healing center, www. bridgeofstars.com

Your Soul, Your Life

A GUIDE TO HEALING AND SELF-HEALING

Your Soul, Your Life

A GUIDE TO HEALING AND
SELF-HEALING

Marzcia Techau

BOOKS

London, UK
Washington, DC, USA

CollectiveInk

First published by O-Books, 2024
O-Books is an imprint of Collective Ink Ltd.,
Unit 11, Shepperton House, 89 Shepperton Road, London, N1 3DF
office@collectiveinkbooks.com
www.collectiveinkbooks.com
www.o-books.com

For distributor details and how to order please visit the 'Ordering' section on our website.

Text copyright: Marzcia Techau, 2021
1st edition
Translated from Danish "Din Sjæl, Dit Liv" by Lotte and David Young

ISBN: 978 1 80341 657 1
978 1 80341 679 3 (ebook)
Library of Congress Control Number: 2023946401

Design: Lapiz Digital Services
Cover, graphic design and illustrations: Christina Bemmann
Author photos: Nikolai Linares

www.marzcia.dk www.facebook.com/marzciashealingscenter

UK: Printed and bound by CPI Group (UK) Ltd, Croydon, CR0 4YY
Printed in North America by CPI GPS partners

We operate a distinctive and ethical publishing philosophy in
all areas of our business, from our global network of authors to
production and worldwide distribution.

CONTENTS

Index Illustrations in the book

In loving memory of Sean Keahi

SYMBOLS USED IN THIS BOOK

■   Karmic blockages from previous lives

●   Epigenetic blockages in the lineage

♥   Blockage resolved

💔   Blockage in the body

∿   Blockage in the soul

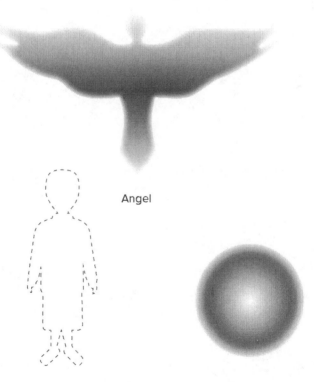

Angel

Deceased relatives and guides   The soul

A LIFE IN ACCORDANCE WITH YOURSELF

You are unique here on Earth. Only you have your body, your feelings, your thoughts and your soul. This book is about all of you, about how to get closer to your soul essence, and about the potential you have to heal yourself. Our soul fills far more than our body and it can radiate into the world, enabling us to fulfil our purpose to the joy of others and ourselves. There can be many paths to a balanced collaboration between body and soul, and I would like to show you some of the ones I have experienced in myself and with others through my work. I have seen how getting rid of beliefs, blockages, and traumas from early childhood, past lives, or lineage through healing can redeem people, make room for their soul essence, and lead to deeply meaningful lives. The spirit world is always ready to help us if we reach out, and I hope this book can inspire you to do so.

Take notice of the talents you have. What do you do that makes you feel good; what gives you peace, joy or meaning? This is often the way your soul expresses its qualities. Notice and think about what you did to have fun, what you got absorbed in or felt like doing, but perhaps never had the opportunity to do when you were a child. This can contain very important information for you about what calling your soul has and what you can do to find your strength, peace, joy and love and thereby get more in touch with yourself and the developmental opportunities you have. I want to give you the opportunity to sense and connect with your own soul essence and brick by brick, blockage by blockage, let your light shine so that your completely unique, luminous path emerges. When we have contact with our innermost essence or our soul, we find it easier to experience the souls of others and the support of the spirit world. We are spiritual beings, and by drawing the spiritual aspect into our lives, we also draw it into the world. The world can be changed and become a place where we live life, rather than a place where we simply survive and are trapped in patterns and habits that inevitably cause us to repeat the same survival strategies.

In this book, the way your nervous system orientates itself according to the outside world will be explained, as well as how this is precisely what enables you to be in contact with a divine presence and receive healing. You will be introduced to different ways of collaborating with the spirit world – karmic, epigenetic and through inner-child work – and you will be given specific methods and exercises for self-healing. You will also read stories from my own life and those of a number of participants in my courses, where blockages or traumas have been resolved with the help of the spirit world and have led to better lives.

I hope that both the theoretical material and the real, lived stories will provide food for thought and inspire you. I don't have the ultimate truth or path for you, but I have suggestions for opportunities to create good contact with your soul and the spirit world. The most important thing for me is that you use what makes sense for you and your life so that you can walk the path of your own soul.

It is your soul and your life.

LIFE'S POSSIBILITIES AND LIMITATIONS

Human life is full of challenges that make it difficult for us to live in accordance with our soul essence. We could also call it our true self or our inner core. The soul essence is that which is you in the purest, non-physical form. The soul has no limitations; it wants everything and can do everything, but it doesn't always get the space it needs when we are physically incarnated. As human beings, we have a number of fantastic possibilities, but we also have limitations; both by virtue of our physical form – we have a body that has its own flaws, gets its diseases and ultimately has to perish – and in the form of our mental or emotional convictions and blockages. Our body and mind are designed to survive and keep us away from dangers, and that is a really good thing in those situations that actually are dangerous – when in the past we had to flee from wild animals, or when we are today in the middle of a dangerous situation in the traffic or at risk of falling down a steep mountainside. But it can also mean that in our ordinary, daily lives, where there is no actual danger, we close off important aspects of ourselves. It happens because we don't return to the feeling of security and ease. Our nervous system doesn't settle down into peace and quiet but stays in a kind of constant state of alarm. Because we experience situations where our surroundings react negatively to us expressing who we are, we may come to believe that it is always dangerous, for example, to be calm or vulnerable or to take our space. And because the body and mind want to protect us from dangers, we gradually close off those sides of ourselves. These are simple survival mechanisms which can either stem from experiences or rejections in this life, or which can be inherited from our lineage (epigenetic) or from the soul's experiences in previous lives (karmic). This book will make suggestions for how to transform and heal these survival mechanisms and unleash your potential to live and survive in the best way possible in accordance with yourself.

HAMSTER WHEEL OR CHAOS

It will also occasionally happen that we restrict and block each other. Most often not out of malice, but because we are individually or together caught in patterns and traumas that, if we don't get them loosened up, cause us to come up against the same problems and challenges over and over again. These patterns may be due to traumas or blockages in this life, traumas that recur in your lineage (epigenetic), or ones that your soul has not finished working on (karmic). Whatever the reason, we all have physical, mental, and emotional autopilots that make us repeat actions, think the same thoughts and create atmospheres that keep us in the same strategies. It may be that your autopilot keeps you in a strategy where you are constantly creating so much external chaos that it prevents you from going in depth with your own internal chaos and getting to grips with what is really going on there.

You simply create a kind of smokescreen so that you don't have to deal with what you don't want to look at because it is too overwhelming or too difficult. It could also be that you live a super-controlled life with everything taped and no room for spontaneous development, close connections, or fun, quirky experiences. You are so afraid of letting go and losing control that you simply become afraid of living, and this can lead to a great deal of loneliness and a lack of presence and sense of life. A third strategy in which many of us modern people get caught up is a stressful everyday life with family, job and a whole load of activities, all of which are superficially good, but the tempo and our lack of presence prevents us from being 100% there in it, recharging for the next day and just enjoying life. We are simply living a life on the run, physically, mentally and emotionally, until we are completely exhausted and numb. This model is also known as "the hamster wheel."

Externally, the three strategies may look very different, but emotionally they are not really that far from the powerlessness of the chaos in the first strategy. At their core, all three strategies are about not really being yourself (or in touch with yourself). Instead of living, you are surviving, rigidly fixed in your blockages.

4

Perhaps you can recognise yourself in one of these three strategies or a mixture of them. And perhaps you are now thinking that you are a bad person for living or having lived like that. But your challenges and blockages have been and are helping to make you who you are, just as much as your abilities and qualities. All three strategies – chaos, control and hamster wheel – are understandable and well-founded. It has made sense for you to live in this way because that is what has worked best for you so far, and it is familiar and safe. It may even be that these strategies still work for you – there is nothing "right" or "wrong." We evolve step by step, in accordance with our development, and it isn't my intention to urge you to push through something. Tenderness and gentleness towards yourself are essential ingredients in your work with yourself and your development.

INCLUDE YOUR SOUL

You are probably used to working with your body, your feelings and your thoughts. But perhaps you need to involve your soul essence and the world your soul comes from, i.e., the spirit world. At least that's how I have experienced it with many of the clients and course participants who have come to me – frustrated at working with the same theme or pattern for a long time. This is where the spirit world and your own soul (which are two sides of the same coin) can help you. In the spirit world, you will find help from your team of guides, your deceased relatives and an infinite divine presence. Your soul is always ready and willing to experience something in this life and enrich the world here and now. But there is much that can bring disturbance and limits into a human life; the body, the feelings and the thoughts can get in the way, so that there isn't really much room for your soul essence to unfold. When there isn't any room for the soul essence, you aren't completely yourself, you aren't completely satisfied and you aren't completely in accordance with who you are. But you can be!

Over the years, I have seen time and again how big a difference it can make in the human life we have here and now to make room for the soul and connect with the help of the spirit world. It helps us heal current, past and lineal trauma, get loosened up and create space. It is like when we clean up at home and throw out old, useless things, gently making room for what needs to grow and have space in the future. Even though I believe that, as souls, we have several lives, the life we have in this incarnation won't come again. I have a life here and now – with my spouse, Jette, my family, my friends and the wonderful people I meet in my work – which is precious and important to me since I know it won't come again exactly like this. Your life here and now is also precious, and you must therefore live it totally and to the full.

YOUR LIGHT IN THE WORLD

My wish with this book is to support you in gaining more access to yourself, your life, your resources, and your inner spiritual strengths and qualities, not just so that you as a human being can get the most out of your life now, for the benefit of yourself, but also because it is of benefit to your loved ones and the community of which you are a part. When your soul has space to radiate out into the world and you live in accordance with your soul essence, you also have the reserves of energy to positively affect your surroundings. When we have contact with our innermost essence, we find it easier to experience the souls of other people and the support of the spirit world. We are spiritual beings, and by involving that spiritual aspect in our lives, we are also involving it in the world. That isn't selfish but loving. Our soul essence isn't ego, it is important, and it must have nourishment to be able to take its space and do good. Through self-care, attention, and responsibility for yourself, you can transform yourself from being a bucket full of holes where all the energy gushes out, to making a start with nourishing yourself so that your core essence begins to radiate. It will always give a better result, not only for you but also for the world because when you are in deficit, your survival mechanisms come into play. I am perfectly sure you know this from when you come home to your family worn out and still clean up after the others or start making dinner, even if you are really hungry and just want to have food served up for you. We do all those things with the best intentions, but we can exhaust ourselves and others in that state because we act on the basis that we think we should be good people, not from a position of genuinely feeling like doing it. That is when we begin to feel overlooked and wronged, and we blame our surroundings for wearing us out.

That is why it is good for everyone when we focus on what helps us flourish. It often happens that the more we get ourselves into balance, the greater capacity and surplus energy we have to share with others. When you are thriving, your insights and your essence come out so clearly that you can be supportive of more people. It is like a tiny seed that has taken in nourishment, grown and become a plant, then becomes a small flower, which eventually bears fruit. In the end, you can share all the fruits and other people can live from them. Although there are many who feel pessimistic right now because of, for example, the state of the climate and all the conflicts in the world, I have all sorts of hope for us human beings. Right now, we have the largest population of people in the world ever, and with all those souls incarnated, we have endless opportunities to heal ourselves, each other and the world.

You can be a part of that, and the good thing is that you already have access to all the help you need. It is there, inside yourself and outside. It is "just" a matter of clearing the blockages so that you can find help and accept it and act from your essence.

A WAKE-UP CALL FROM A CAR WRITE-OFF

A few years ago, I thought I had found my dream place to both live and work. It was a large estate called Bonderup Manor, near Korsør, which Jette and I rented and lived in, and from where I also ran my business. I thought that here I would be able to both find the peace I hadn't had in the city and expand my work. The last part was true. We had no less than 800 square metres to romp around in, and the business grew as I had dreamt it would because I now had the space for it. I could just get started on whatever I felt like doing. There was also the peace of nature, as the place was surrounded by a large, park-like garden. I thus had a place with opportunities to unfold, but there was still not quite the peace I needed. Such a large place requires maintenance, and there were estate workers who came and worked every day, just as there were ordinary people who came by just to see the estate. Peace and simplicity are important for my ability to concentrate on what I do, and I wasn't getting that at Bonderup, even though I got a lot of other things I had dreamt of. After some deliberations, Jette and I therefore chose to move back to Copenhagen but continue with the teaching out in the countryside. I couldn't afford to carry out the plans I had for the business in Copenhagen, where rents are much higher. It was true that I had seen a place in Copenhagen that could work well, but the rent was far too high, and the landlord demanded that I rent all four floors, which I couldn't afford. Even though I actually had a feeling I was going to celebrate my 50th birthday in that place when I first saw it, I had to say no and continue commuting between town and country. I was now driving back and forth from our home in Copenhagen to my workplace in Bonderup. It was over 100 kilometres each way and sometimes I had to spend the night down there. All in all, the new arrangement meant a lot of separation and a lot of transportation time. But I kept going.

One day, when I was on my way to Bonderup to hold an angel-healing course, I made really strong contact with some of the angels I was going to work with that day. I asked them to resolve my situation in a good way, and immediately felt a great calm inside me. I was told that everything was brilliant and that I could allow myself to be confident in what was going on right now. I therefore drove on happily, arrived in the countryside, parked the car and started teaching.

During the break, a course participant came up to me and said, "Marzcia, your car looks a little strange."

"Well yes," I replied, "it has a few scratches, it will be going to the workshop soon."

Then another participant came over and said, "You know, some of the panels are sticking out strangely."

I thought that sounded a bit odd, so I went out and had a look. It turned out that I had parked the car without applying the handbrake, and it had rolled down a slope in the park and had so much damage it was a write-off. The interesting thing was that it could have rolled straight ahead where there wouldn't have been any problems. Or it could have rolled a little more to the right, and then it would also have finished up in a place where there wouldn't have been any problems. But instead, it had rolled a little upwards over a grassy ridge, down the slope and into a small thicket with a tiny tree. It was a fairly large SUV with top safety – it looked almost like a jeep – but it hit, within a few millimetres, the exact spot where it fell apart. When I went over to the car and saw what had happened, I immediately realised that I would be moving the business back to Copenhagen, because I was completely dependent on the car to get back and forth, and inside myself I said quietly, "It's about time I let go of Bonderup and find other paths."

I had actually imagined that I would be out in the country for ten years – that had been my plan. That was why I hadn't immediately moved the business to Copenhagen when we moved back there to live, and I also think that was why I would have continued to commute the long way every day if the car hadn't rolled down the slope. Admittedly, it was me who had failed to apply the handbrake, but I have no doubt that the incident was a help to me from my own soul and the spirit world of which it is a part – a vociferous one of its kind, for I hadn't been good at listening until then. I had been so enthused with the plan I thought I should follow, even though I wasn't really thriving on it. Now, surprisingly, it happened that we got a lot of money back from the insurance. Actually, the car had lost a lot in value since we bought it, but since it was a rare model, we got so much in compensation that there was enough to make the downpayment on a new car: even an electric car that I had long wanted for its environmentally friendly engineering – an important feature for me, as I am a biologist by training. An electric car had previously been completely out of my reach, but now it suddenly became possible anyway, not because I was pushing and struggling, but all by itself, as a result of something that had started out looking like an accident. Not long after, it also became possible for me to come back to Copenhagen with my business in a good way. About six months after the incident, I was sitting meditating. I came into state of calmness and got the feeling I needed to contact the place I had earlier been interested in renting. I also had an amount in my head which I would say that I was willing to pay in rent. I contacted the place and it turned out that two of the floors had now been rented out, which meant I could have the floors I wanted at a price I could afford. I quickly moved to Copenhagen in the space of a few months, even though I had originally planned to wait five or six more years. Perhaps I could have listened to my inner voice a little earlier without it having to happen so forcefully, but there was also an advantage in it taking its time, because during that period, the place in which I was interested had become vacant and the rent lowered. That way, it all ended up falling into place in the best possible way.

TRUST AND PATIENCE

For me, the above story illustrates how when I follow the path and the guidance that my soul and the spirit world show me, opportunities open up that I could never have imagined. There is a strong current that supports me, and when I am connected to it, really good things often happen. But connection requires trust and patience – and it also requires conscious action from me. I could have chosen to think that it was awful that my car had fallen apart. Instead, I used the experience to set in motion the actions that I had probably inwardly known for a long time were necessary, but which I hadn't really been able to actualize. In that way, I had to both listen inwardly and take affirmative action outwardly – and know when it was time for the one or the other. When I don't trust the flow, path or movement of life, I am a very restless person who wants everything to happen quickly, or the restlessness gets me into a somewhat stuck state where I don't see and choose the new paths or possibilities that don't fit precisely into the plan I have determined with my will and control. That restlessness is known to many of us modern human beings, and it can easily cause us to make hasty decisions where we don't give ourselves the time to be aware and come in harmony with ourselves. On the other hand, when I have confidence in the path, or the flow, I also have the patience to let things take the time they need. Long before my car fell apart, I knew full well that I wasn't completely happy with where I was geographically, but I didn't really know what should happen instead. The time that passed before things got resolved ended up working for me in the long run. But the time and patience to wait required from

11

me a great deal of trust in the process – the trust that I was told by the angels that I could easily have. It can be demanding to trust the process, but it is important. Sometimes it will feel as if nothing is happening, but it is. Sometimes you might have doubts because you aren't used to believing in something you can't see. Once you have the trust, it also becomes easier to decide when to stay and fight for something, and when it is better to let go and find another way. Many of us have been taught that life is hard and that it is a struggle. But we can actually choose for ourselves when the fight is positive and has a positive effect on us – teaching us something or bringing us to a new, good place – and when it is destructive, and we have to lay down our arms and leave.

By and large, we always have a choice in terms of which paths we follow. This is important for me to emphasise. There isn't one path, but there are probably some paths that are better for you than others. Nevertheless, there may be good reasons for choosing paths for shorter periods of time that are not completely in accordance with who you are. You may have to put yourself in a less than good situation and, if you do it consciously and take care of the pain it triggers in you to do so, something good may well come out of it. That is how it was for a long time when I was commuting. The situation wasn't optimal, but there were compelling reasons to both stay and move. During that period, I had lots of worried thoughts: Can I move the business again? You can't just move a business all the time, surely. What about the plan I have laid out? What will people think? In the end, I just couldn't get to what was right for me through a thinking process; I needed to listen to my soul essence and the help of the spirit world. And then, patiently and with trust, act on what I had heard. It is thus perfectly okay not to always take the "right" path. Life can get in the way, other people can get in the way, and you may not be ready in yourself to take it. But if you live a life where you consistently don't listen to yourself, you may end up getting to a place where you constantly push yourself aside. This is where you can end up getting stressed or maybe "just" wake up one day and think, "What happened to my life?"

You always have an inner capacity to change your perception of yourself and your life, and there is endless help to be found when you make contact with your soul and give yourself the space to live based on your soul essence and your qualities. This book is about how you can use the access to your soul's innermost, authentic essence and being to contact and receive support and guidance from your deceased lineage, the spirit world, and your soul wisdom. Equally important is an understanding of how you have access to a great potential for self-healing through your body. Understanding more about your autonomic nervous system, your biological senses and the structural and developmental stages of your brain throughout childhood can together give you a much greater opportunity to regulate your nervous system and find peace.

HOW TO USE THIS BOOK

It is my sincere desire to pass on my practical experiences and the methods I have developed during my years as a practising spiritual medium, healer and clairvoyant, especially the healing methods of working with the karmic/past lives, the epigenetic/ lineage, reactivation and deactivation, as well as the healing of the inner child, through which I have seen lots of people develop themselves over time. Through my background as a biologist, I draw on recognised theories about the cells, the nervous system, traumas and the effect of healing on various conditions. Among other things, I am interested in Bruce Lipton's theories about intelligent cells, Peter A. Levine's shock/trauma therapy and Michael Newton's work on reincarnation and the wanderings of the soul, just as I draw on teaching that I have received from the Hawaiian healer Sean Keahi, other spiritual teachers over time and not least my daily cooperation with the spirit world and my clients and course participants.

The theories and methods are merely tools; they are a means to illustrate how we function as human beings and as spiritual beings. The most important thing for me is to convey that you always have an infinite help and how to find it within yourself and in the spirit world and the life you are living to create precisely the life that is good for you.

***

Your life, your soul.

CHAPTER 1

BODY, FEELINGS, THOUGHTS
AND SOUL

*About our four planes, their mutual alignment
and readiness for development*

You live with your body somewhere on Earth now, specifically and physically. Even though, in my daily work, I am intensely engaged with the life of the soul and have a strong contact with the spirit world, I am of the conviction that if we focus exclusively on the soul, we miss what is intensely precious in being here physically now. Being a soul incarnated in a body is a unique possibility which – as far as we know – only exists here on Earth. That is why every incarnation is unique and precious.

***

For me, the process of developing ourselves is about the wholeness between the four planes we contain as human beings:

1) **The physical plane:** the physical body, the nervous system and the sensory system
2) **The mental plane:** thoughts and beliefs
3) **The emotional plane:** moods and states
4) **The soul essence/awareness**, including:
   a) Divine essence/awareness
   b) Mental awareness/the beliefs we have from previous lives/mental experience
   c) Emotional awareness from previous lives/emotional experiences

The soul contains the possibility of accommodating and embracing the other planes, and a mutually positive exchange between the planes will strengthen your ability to be master of your life.

A blockage on one plane can limit mastery of your life or can cause you to switch into merely surviving rather than living a full life. Such a blockage will often affect the other planes.

THE SPIRITS PROVIDE GROUNDING

Over the years, I have realised that the more unified I am on the four planes, the more connected I become to my physical life. It might sound like a contradiction to say that the spirit world gives me grounding, but establishing a strong contact to something that many don't regard as down-to-earth, namely the non-physical world, has given me the possibility of establishing myself physically in this life. The contact with my guardian angel, my guide team and deceased pets and my lineage has helped me to settle into my body, in the place I am now – as the human being Marzcia and as a spouse, healer and teacher. In order to draw on the help of the spirit world, we must understand how we human beings function.

As living human beings, we consist of a body in the form of a skeleton, organs, blood vessels, muscles, skin, a brain, a nervous system and so on. We are living, complex organisms with a whole system within us that works most of the time without us noticing it. We don't notice that there is a system that can experience defects or definite meltdown until the body gives us signals that something is awry, gets injured or completely malfunctions. The body can accommodate feelings such as anger, joy, love, solicitude, fear, disappointment and jealousy. We get to know them from quite a young age, and we learn – if we have good adults around us – to identify and be with the feelings that are present in a good way. Finally, we often have a lot of thoughts in our head; a mental plane that often governs our actions. This plane, especially in our era, is very overprioritised; we modern humans try to think our way to most solutions in our lives. This means that many of us live mostly based on thoughts and beliefs, and ignore our feelings and the sensations and signals we get from our bodies.

Others get trapped in their feelings without noticing that many of the feelings go round in circles, just as thoughts do, and that they are in fact not particularly good as guides alone; the body tries to hold everything together because this is where we are – the body is the container for our feelings and thoughts.

The soul is the fourth plane. It connects you with the spirit world. All our souls are connected, just as your cells are connected and form your body, or as the drops in the sea are each themselves and together form a sea. The soul is always there, just like your feelings, your thoughts and your body. You always have a small flame inside you that shines and that is full of desire to experience and contribute. But there isn't always very much space for the soul. You may have blockages in your body, feelings or thoughts that get in the way, tightening and restricting so that your soul essence can't reach out to you or you can't reach into it. Maybe you can't even really sense it.

WHEN THE FOUR PLANES COLLABORATE

Your body and your nervous system remember everything you have experienced, from before your birth to who you are today. You may have repressed some of it, or you may bear experiences from before you acquired language and a more functioning memory or consciousness. The soul consciousness has a basis of divine essence, comprising both mental states and emotional states. It is always connected with the spirit world. In addition, the soul contains beliefs and feelings from past lives. In short, your soul consciousness contains your innermost essence and the potentials, qualities and resources you have with you in this life. Your soul consciousness can cooperate with your body, thoughts and feelings in your life. Your nervous system is designed to orientate itself to the atmospheres and states you are surrounded by and the states you experience within yourself.

THE FOUR PLANES

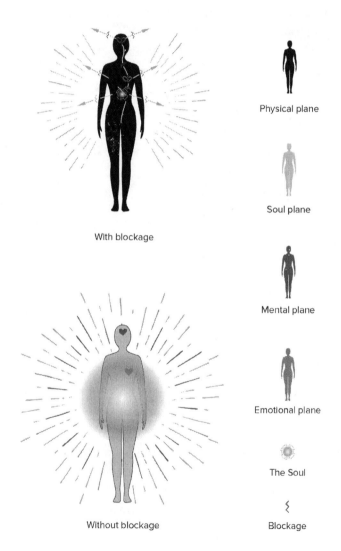

With blockage

Without blockage

Physical plane

Soul plane

Mental plane

Emotional plane

The Soul

Blockage

The nervous system is in this way the link between your body and your soul. When you are in contact with your soul, there is calm, wisdom, love and surplus energy, and when the nervous system registers that contact, it will convey the states throughout the body. Then positive feedback is formed from the calm in the soul to the calm in the nervous system, and you have a relaxed and safe bodily experience. This in turn will enhance the experience of calm and security. You steadily gain access to your soul and the resources and capabilities you have. There will often be experiences of expanding, radiating out into the world, standing strong, loving and opening in yourself. Your contact to your essence will be better, and that will mean that you become more and more present with yourself and others. Your choices will be made based on a safe, strong, loving and wise place within you, a vivid life.

THE NERVOUS SYSTEM IN FEAR

When you are stressed or have negative feelings and thoughts about yourself and life, your nervous system will register the situation and start telling your body that there is danger looming. Your body goes into survival mode and you find it difficult to get in touch with the calming aspect of your soul. You lose some of the contact with your soul essence and end up with a more pressurised, stressed nervous system, where life is about survival, fear and parts of you shutting down. Your choices are being made on the basis of survival mechanisms – you are surviving, but not living. The survival mechanisms are good when you need to save yourself from short-term danger situations and if there is a good dynamic between calming, restful, secure and pressurised or dangerous situations. It is a very positive thing to have a healthy nervous system that can activate quickly, but also quickly return to rest, security and a more conscious contact to your soul essence.

The problem arises if your system or parts of your system can't come down to a good, safe state of rest and return to living instead of "merely" surviving. Then it is going to limit your chances of being in touch with the best version of yourself. In this way, your sensory system and your nervous system have been developed to often be unconsciously very aware of your surroundings and inner states. When you are safe, your nervous system is also safe and has more "surplus" to sense more nuances of life. These early imprints from your childhood sit very deep in your nervous system and in your ways of reacting.

The body has many important functions and without it we would not be alive in the physical world. It connects directly back to the animals and the earliest forms of life, and that is important to keep in mind. Our nervous systems have elements from organisms in the primordial ocean, reptiles, mammals and primates. Our brains are threefold and consist of:

1) Our thinking brain (neocortex)
2) The sensory, social brain (the mammalian brain)
3) Instinct and survival (the reptile brain)

This threefold division is crucial to our reactions and survival strategies, and the better we understand it, the better we will understand our sensory apparatus and be able to accept ourselves and each other. Our body is a system designed for survival, and if something is too overwhelming to be processed and healed at once, our system will find ways to move forward anyway. Throughout our lives, we all have different experiences that have left their mark on us. Some of them inhibit us, others strengthen us. If you want to show the world more and more of who you are and get what's blocking you in your life weeded out, it is important to become aware of what you do and why you do it. Why you think the way you think. Why you feel the way you feel. In that process, you will begin to experience that you aren't only your body, your thoughts and your feelings, but that you also have your soul-essence consciousness. The more you come in contact with your innermost essence, the more peace, clarity, love and strength you get in touch with. The soul is the plane that can accommodate and support the other three planes. It holds everything together and creates an inner fellowship of acceptance and inclusiveness within you and also in your way of perceiving the world. I believe that we live many times and that after each incarnation, we have some very educational looks at previous lives so that we can better decide what we want to learn and impart in the coming life. Your soul has wisdom, potential and qualities with it as well as a great desire to contribute to the world it is stepping into. The soul contains the radiant consciousness you are. It contains a divine part, which is consciousness, mental and emotional states, but also beliefs and emotional states from the experiences of past lives.

I always teach my clairvoyance students to start by getting a sense of the client's soul essence, because the soul essence is our life energy (not our survival energy). It is the place in us where we are the clearest, most loving, purest, calmest and wisest part of ourselves. Once the light in the individual is seen or felt, it is very easy to see where the person's essence has been blocked or restrained from radiating out into the world and manifesting itself.

Once you have grasped the cause of the blockage and asked for help with that specifically, you will find that the healing process or insights come easier and that more of your energy, light and resources are released. Imagine that the physical tension contains something hidden which your mental or emotional plane hasn't been prepared to handle or process at the time it arose. Your body remembers and stores and delivers whatever may be there. You therefore move the focus away from that which is difficult to handle, to that which is easier to relate to and carry on with. Of course, there are illnesses and physical conditions that are neither psychologically nor mentally based. Sometimes a broken arm is just a broken arm, and the flu is just the flu. We are born and we die, and we often die of illnesses. That, and the fact that we are all going to move on from here, is also something we need to relate to and accept. I write this to emphasise that I don't think it is our own fault that we get ill. On the other hand, I think that everything we experience is part of a process for which our soul and our development are prepared. What we do with that learning, and the insights that have the possibility of emerging, is what we learn and grow from.

The better the connectedness and collaboration you have between the four planes, the more you are in contact with the qualities that each plane contains. A good balance between the four planes strengthens your contact with the physical life you are living, your everyday life, your intuition and the guidance you are getting from the spirit world. As we have seen, a blockage or imbalance in one of the planes will affect the others, and therefore it is important to take care of the challenges that exist and appreciate the good qualities that each plane has.

FAREWELL TO RESEARCH – HELLO TO (MORE OF) THE SOUL

For me, it has been the case that I have been most pressurised physically, mentally and emotionally when I have been at university and in research environments. Some years ago, I had to say farewell to this part of my life and it turned into a hello to something completely different to what I had anticipated. The story shows something about how important the balance between the four planes is – and that we can get so much out of balance that it takes a forceful incident to pull us back.

I originally trained and qualified as a biologist and love being where something happens and where people are driven to create change through researching, understanding and going in depth with that about which they are passionate. There is something very inspiring about the university and research world that has really been and still is an important part of my curiosity about life and the physical and spirit worlds. The problem for me is that it is at the same time a very brain-dominated environment, and that it often isn't possible to go as much in depth with topics and have as much time for the individual parts as I would like. There is a tough and intense race for research grants; it is all about coming first, and the competition is fierce. Under such pressure, I have many times shut off too much of myself and used my will and fighting spirit at the expense of my health, my couple relationships and my social relationships. Today that is over, and it ended with a bang – literally.

The last time I was employed at the university was in 2013. I had just done the recordings for the programme *The Spirits Return* on TV3+, and I was in the process of writing my first book, *When The Spirits Come Calling*. At the same time, I was writing research articles and processing data from a research project. In short, I had many pots on the stove. In October, a month before my book was to be published, my two-year employment contract with the university was about to expire. At this very moment, at the beginning of an angel-healing course I was holding, I happened to open a cupboard door directly into my right eye and the bridge of my nose. It really hurt and triggered a lot of symptoms that probably should have got my alarm bells ringing: I couldn't remember how to spell my course participants' names, and I had headaches, nausea and car-sickness tendencies. I had had concussions in the past, so I should definitely have kept myself completely still. But that was precisely what I didn't do. I ignored all the signals because I had articles to write, interviews to give, photo sessions to be held,

TV appearances, a book fair, PR and much more. I thought it was just a little knock from a cupboard door. After three weeks, however, my symptoms had only got worse, and finally I had to lie down quietly in a dark room for several days. But it was too late. The damage had been done. I could no longer multi-task and I couldn't do any planning. The process of looking several steps forward in time became a huge effort for me, which caused a kind of brain and system meltdown in me every time I tried. This meant that I didn't finish writing the research articles that I was doing; instead, I had to leave them to some co-authors, which was quite an effort and a sorrow. I could neither read, write nor understand anything I tried to read. I felt completely useless and all my mental sharpness had vanished. A path I had for years followed and fought for was suddenly shut down forever. In my own business, I tried to get through the daily administrative and practical tasks, but my symptoms didn't go away. After about a year, I had to accept that I could no longer do it all myself, and began to get help from assistants for many of the things that were no longer possible for me to do myself, or which simply demanded too much effort from me.

The following years were intense for me. I had to learn to use myself in a new way, especially learning to let go and delegate work tasks. It certainly wasn't easy. I experienced a great deal of sadness and a sense of powerlessness. I felt unsuccessful, weak, and devastated, and I had a really hard time letting go of my old way of being me. Like many others, I had been used to being able to do things myself and wanting to do things myself, so giving up parts of my work to create space for the peace I suddenly needed was a huge challenge. In hindsight, I had needed more peace long before the cupboard door hit the bridge of my nose, but I hadn't managed to make space for that peace because of the fear of what would happen if I took time off. I had had worrying thoughts like: Can people manage without me being involved all the time? Will everything now fall apart?

What about all that desire burning within me and wanting to come out, to make a difference in the world, is it over? … and suchlike. Now I didn't have any choice. After the concussion, I simply had to get better at deciding what to agree to and what not to agree to. There was a tangible settling of accounts because if I didn't do what my body needed, I would feel bad, both physically and mentally. As soon as I didn't keep my focus on calm, centring in the body and a deep inner slowness, I started spinning around like a spinning top in my head, and it caused a meltdown in my system.

So, in the years after the bang on the nose, I had to agree to say farewell to the dream of a Ph.D. in research on the effects of healing, while at the same time I had to cut back on work tasks in my own business. I had to think in terms of making things easier for myself and, above all, asking for help. I went to several doctors, neurologists and different types of therapists, just as I performed healing on myself. One of the neurologists said that I had to be "optimistically patient" with the process. For a live wire like me who is very happy when things are going quickly, this was incredibly difficult. But I had to do it. It was as if everything inside me had got jammed and I had to maintain a slowness and a constant focus on my footing every day in order to keep my feelings of seasickness and nausea at bay.

DEVELOPMENT IS DIFFICULT – HELP IS CLOSE AT HAND

Such a transition is definitely not pleasant. But not only bad things happened to me. For example, the interesting thing that happened was that now that my brain couldn't handle very much any more, now that the clarity, sharpness and planning part of my activities had been reduced and I had delegated tasks that drained me, my other senses and spiritual competence grew. Because I constantly had to focus on feeling whether I was at peace or what it took for me to get down into my body from my head, my contact with myself and the spirit world became stronger. It makes sense because my job as a medium is to be a channel and not use my brain in an everyday thinking mode. I use my system in a completely different way, where it is the senses, the intuition, the body and the inner images and impulses that make up the communication between me, the spirit world and the client. Everything for which we human beings normally use our brains is not part of the job I have. The healings, courses and clairvoyance all went really well too. I felt (and still feel) good when I worked with the spirit world. I was in a state of inner peace and I got lots of healing myself during that period. On the other hand, I had a hard time when I had to have the first clairvoyance evening with a deceased contact after the blow to the nose. It was as if I couldn't get the images and information I received down into my heart, to my clairsentience and intuitive sense of what should be said, what the information meant, and so on. It was really anxiety-provoking to be facing an audience and lack one of the most important tools in my work with contacting the deceased. I barely got through the evening and was very unsure whether or not I could work as a medium any longer. Again, I became worried: Should both my research and my deceased contact now go phut because of a tiny knock?

The next clairvoyance session was six weeks off, and during that time I chose to visit a very experienced English spiritual medium. She told me that she saw me doing my next clairvoyance evening at something that resembled a hotel and that it would go well. I breathed a sigh of relief, because my next clairvoyance evening was at a guest house in a provincial town south of Copenhagen. She also said that, over the course of their lives, all spiritual mediums experience their abilities changing and new ways of collaborating with the spirit world emerge. The session with her gave me the peace of mind to face what was happening to me more positively and open myself to the changes that were going on. The clairvoyance evening went well and I have had lots of clairvoyance evenings since.

This is often what is so challenging for us when we are developing; we can easily feel what we are losing, but we don't know yet what we will get instead, and that can be frightening. Accepting the new conditions when our physical and mental state changes can be terribly difficult. It was very stressful for me in those years to have confidence in the process and positive awareness of what was opening up, rather than falling into the trap of crying over my lost opportunities and skills. I was also struggling with anger at myself over the fact that a silly little accident had changed my life in a few seconds and that I was even to blame for it myself because I was too busy and hadn't been paying attention. This is how it can go for all of us in developmental processes, and here the spirit world can help, not by walking the path for us, but by supporting us in the fact that we are on the right path – as the visit to the English medium, for example, had shown me. And the help is always there.

BREAKTHROUGH AND LEARNING

It took four years, in which I felt that I had been optimistically patient for a very long time, before I began to notice cognitive improvements generally and specific improvements in terms of being able to read. At that time, I had adapted to my new situation and accepted that this was just the way things were. Then a combination of "coincidences" meant that I started with an osteopath who referred me to an optometrist, and I started the SE programme.[1] My physical training combined with the trauma work had the effect of suddenly giving me a big breakthrough. The therapists discovered that my optic nerve to the right eye had been damaged, and that I was therefore compensating for it and using so much concentration and energy there that my brain was shutting down from overexertion. After some intense work with exercises, treatments, physical training and trauma work, I finished up in a completely different place.

Today I feel much better and can manage much more, but I am still not going back to university and research. The learning I got from my injury is important for me to hold on to so that I don't end up being an overly busy little Duracell bunny again, driving my own system to the limit of total exhaustion, because that's not what I am supposed to be doing.

The concussion was obviously not something I wanted, but I can say today that I have undergone a development that I am sure I wouldn't have undergone if I hadn't been forced to slow down. The blow forced me to learn to delegate work tasks, find greater inner peace, and switch to a slower tempo. I can still occasionally have a sinking feeling over having to say goodbye to my beloved research and give up being buried in reading for hours on end, which I also enjoyed intensely. When that happens, I fortunately also remember everything that has been opened up and how the spirit world has taken me through to a whole different level, both professionally and privately. I needed to get away from the mental work and immerse myself more in myself, my private life and, in general, work to strengthen myself, so that I could become an even better channel for the spirit world and develop my spiritual abilities. I can see that clearly now, but along the way it wasn't always clear and at times I was in a total fog.

BETTER AFTER THE CRISIS

This is how it is to be in development; we sometimes feel that we are losing direction, that we are losing our old selves without having fully gained access to our new selves yet, and it is a frustrating process.

It is a bit like a plant standing in a pot with insufficient, depleted soil and needing to be replanted. This transplantation period – getting used to the new soil, the bigger pot, the new conditions and surroundings – takes time, but after that process, the plant has a better root system, new growth and health. Many of my course participants and clients have been in accidents or had illnesses or autoimmune diseases and have therefore been forced to stop and look at their lives. Their environment and their body have, so to speak, forced them to slow down or completely stop their express trains.

Out of this, many different phases emerge:1) The emergency brake, where everything is slowed down or stopped2) The acceptance of what has happened3) The regeneration where the new life is to be built4) The embrace of the new, where a new everyday life finds its rhythm and form5) The maintenance and development of the new.

That is how it was for me too with the blow to the head. I went through all the phases before I got back in place. It wasn't a pleasant journey, but I have arrived at a better place. I dreamt of changing the world by doing research in healing, and I still find it really exciting how healing can help affect health. I thought that if I researched in the area, I could help spread it and integrate it into health care and society. But I can't do any more research. I thus had to figure out something else, and it turned out to be even more of what I wanted. For example, I do morning healing and a guided meditation from half past seven to eight every morning. There are 100 people in my group. Many of them report back that they experience far better peace and contact with themselves and their lives. It may well be that my ideas and my knowledge of healing don't come in as an integral part of health care in this life, but the changing light I feel every morning is far greater. Moving away from the world of research and committing myself even more to being a spiritual person has given me a better life and a better opportunity to do what I am here for: being myself and letting the spirit world support what is to happen: follow, listen and then act. I make myself available as a channel for the light, knowing full well that I also have a responsibility for my own life as a human being. When I am thriving, I have more energy to give to others.

My experience with the concussion is far from unique. People often feel better after a crisis than they had felt before. They value life, themselves and their fellow human beings even more than before. However, I don't think we need to move so far away from ourselves that it takes a hard blow to the head to get us "back in place." We "just" need to get better at following our intuition and listening to all parts of us long before things go wrong so that we can adjust faster. That requires that we learn to get the body, the mind, the feelings and the soul to collaborate. A good balance between the four planes strengthens your contact with the physical life you are living, your everyday life, your intuition and guidance from the spirit world. If there is a blockage or imbalance in one of the planes, it will affect the other planes. You know this from everyday life, where a pain in the foot affects your mood and the way you think about yourself. Or nervousness before an exam gives you a stomach ache or perspiration on the forehead. You also experience it positively when a reciprocated falling-in-love experience gives you butterflies in the stomach, joy and a mass of positive thoughts about how amazing this world really is. In this way, the connection is quite natural and obvious to us on a daily basis, but when we have to solve our big problems in life, we don't always find it easy to think holistically. We get tunnel vision and focus on one of the planes, but we don't solve the problems in the others, and then the blockage will remain. If we have back pain, we focus on exercises and training but forget to look at stress and emotional strain. If we have a problem at work, we try to use our thought process to solve it but ignore the signals from our bodies and the feelings in play between us and our colleagues. It is therefore important that we both take care of the challenges we may have on each plane and value the good qualities that each plane has. It isn't enough for us to be in good physical shape and exercise if our thoughts constantly revolve around how bad we are at something or how much more we ought to be achieving in life. It isn't enough either that we try to think our way to the solution to our problems if we don't anchor those solutions in our feelings and our bodies – because then they just come back, maybe even worse than before.[2] And just as our bodies need nourishment, water and exercise, and our emotional and mental lives need stimulation, our souls also need space, nourishment and light. There must be a balance in the four planes if you are going to feel well.

READINESS

Just as we operate on four planes, there are also four degrees of how ready we are for development. We can be physically ready, mentally ready, emotionally ready and soul-ready. In relation to the soul, we can speak of a soul readiness, but many times it is more about whether we are ready to say yes to the soul. The soul is always ready.

It may also be that society isn't ready, even if the individual is. When the witch-burnings took place in the middle-ages, for example, society wasn't prepared for women to have strength; there was a need for the church or the masculine force to maintain a position of power. Throughout history, forward thinkers have fought battles and created movements in the society in which they lived. They have stood as shining lights and have been at the forefront of developments that have only much later spread to society and moved it forward. In the development of all societies, there have been some people who have walked the path and set the movement in motion, often with great sacrifices for the individual as a result.

When I talk about readiness here, however, it is about the individual – about you and your readiness to develop yourself and bring yourself more in accordance with who you are. It requires a readiness on all planes. You can be physically ready, but not mentally ready. Or mentally ready, but not emotionally ready. There is often a predominance of readiness on one of the planes, and this is exactly where many people can get frustrated. "I've been to a psychologist and worked with it," they say, for example, about a certain theme that comes up over and over again. And it is certainly good to work with your thoughts and beliefs, but if they don't reach the body and the feelings, we won't fully succeed. For example, it may be that you grew up in a divorce family and you have therefore built up a lack of trust in couple relationships and you think that you can't trust anyone where love is concerned. You may have gone to a psychologist and worked on the mental plane to solve your problem with trust, and you may have also gained some clear understanding of yourself, but they haven't really sunk into your nervous system, into your body and into your feelings as being brought to completion. The next point will be that you can really feel that you are comfortable with your partner, or you can feel like you have to surrender to love because it won't disappear again. When we work with ourselves, we have to feel if the work has sunk in mentally, physically and emotionally. Is it just thoughts and beliefs, or has it sunk into the feelings and the body as well? Many of my course participants become deeply frustrated when they feel they have been working on the same issues for ten years and feel that they don't really feel up to going into it again. But it is precisely the reluctance to go in there that shows that it isn't finished.

If, on the other hand, you listen to your body, you automatically enter your thoughts and feelings and become aware that, for example, it is important that you become less stressed, think more positively, allow yourself to have rest and peace and enjoy being in your life. If the body enjoys being in life, the rest does too. In this way, the four planes are connected.

As we will see later, healing supports your readiness. It isn't about daring, and it isn't about pressurising yourself to be ready – on the contrary. You need to lovingly, gently and patiently take care of something that is very vulnerable; it shouldn't be pressed through. The wonderful thing about the gentle approach is that as soon as you make room for something that is truly vulnerable, it becomes strong. Whereas if you push and repress, then you maintain your fragility. It is therefore important that you treat yourself gently. On many occasions, we turn anxiety and pressure against ourselves, often because we have experienced and heard criticism from the outside; we have heard that we aren't good enough and that we are worthless, and then we start playing that same song inside. We actually create an unloving environment for ourselves. Growth is thus about noticing what we say about ourselves, what we say to ourselves, and what we think and feel about ourselves. You will often be affected by some experiences that you have with you from your childhood; the self-same experiences of not being good enough, strong enough, quick enough, etc. You can also have self-esteem issues with you epigenetically, from your lineage, or karmically, from your soul, and you can also work with that, with joy not only in this life, but also in the past and the future – your life and others'. When we become aware of all that we are carrying with us, it also changes our ability to receive help. Many of us have been used to the fact that there was no help to be had, so it takes something to be able to accept help when it is suddenly there. For example, if you are a highly sensitive person and you have landed in a family where there was no surplus energy for you to learn how to handle having a sensitive nervous system and a rich inner life, then you may have experienced seeking help but not getting it. You have made your tentative approaches and they haven't been accepted, or you may even have been rejected or, even worse, made wrong. When you open up to the help and see that it is there, you also open up for a return visit to all the times when it was not there and it can fill you with sadness. In this way, development is hard work that requires great compassion and gentleness with yourself.

If you are ready on all four planes at once, the development is usually really fast, and you can often see it by the fact that great things are happening on both the inner and outer planes. It is like a seed that has accumulated lots of nourishment for a long time and eventually sprouts and blooms. You have accumulated the resources, the conditions are in your favour, and now you can grow really quickly, often with very big changes. It could be that you change jobs, open up to new relationships and close off old ones. You find out what you want with your life, and trust that it can be done.

BUT HOW DO YOU GET TO THIS BEAUTIFUL PLACE?

Here is where the soul comes into the picture. As a healer, I see people on a daily basis who are trapped in the power of their feelings, bodies or thoughts. I help them get in touch with their soul essence, where there is always peace. When this happens, the self-healing potential of the soul essence is activated and you can begin to help yourself. The help of the spirit world is mental, emotional, and physical. Those who are healed notice that within them there is something that has all the qualities they need and that they have something good to contribute. Our blockages and beliefs can lead us to believe that we aren't good enough, that we have no energy, or that other people will never understand us anyway. When you come in contact with your soul essence, you come in contact with something that will always support you. It gives you the strength to work on emotionally, mentally or physically difficult issues. As a healer, I work to help people achieve oneness with their soul essence. From there, they can then begin to work with themselves, unleash their self-healing potential on all four planes, and become able to receive the love and support that is within human beings and outside from the physical world and the spirit world.

***

Laura's story:
'I HAVE TURNED MY LIFE AROUND 180 DEGREES'

Laura, now 28 years old, had struggled with depression, anxiety and stress all her life, when one day she went to a clairvoyance evening armed with scepticism. The evening set in motion a development that has changed everything from Laura's outlook on life to her trouser size and has given her the joy of waking up to her life.

"I have always had to work hard to have a sense of feeling well. In my teens, I had to resort to psychologists and other therapists because I had both depression and anxiety. The first time I went to a psychologist, I was seventeen, but I've had the feeling for as long as I can remember: that there was like some kind of bell jar between me and others, and I felt lonely. It was as if I had to fight more than I should, just to feel ordinarily good. The happy pills didn't work, and even though the psychologists were kind, I never quite got completely 'above water.' I thought about everything too much and I was having a difficult time.

I only just made it through high school and later trained as a social educator to work with children and young people. When I was newly qualified, I got a job in forensic psychiatry, where I worked in a closed ward for mentally ill criminals. The work was totally draining. It was stressful because it was busy and violent situations could arise even if you tried to avoid them. But the work environment and the heavy energies that were around also affected me.

So I broke down with stress after twenty months. It was September, and I was just sitting on my sofa staring at my white wall because that was all I could manage. In general, I have always been an inquisitive, nerdy person who, for example, loved philosophy. Now all that was gone. I was empty.

New year, new life

After a three-month absence, I was fired from my job, and that was good because I was quite simply unable to work. I couldn't even cook for myself. Everything was a mess and running on repeat. I could watch the same film four times in one day because I forgot it after each time. My boyfriend didn't really understand me and I broke up with him during that period.

When New Year arrived, I said to myself that this was going to be a new year and a new life. New year, new life, I repeated to myself like a mantra. At one point, I knew I needed to get out of the house and find something entertaining, and I found a clairvoyance evening at the local library. I had never heard of a clairvoyance evening before, but it only cost 150 kroner, and I thought it sounded cheap to 'get back into the circus.' Such was my attitude.

On the evening itself, my mother and I sat in the back row because we wouldn't enjoy attracting attention, but the medium pointed us out and told us that a deceased man was coming through who wanted to talk to either my mother or me. He also related some very specific details about the man's tools but, unfortunately, we were too closed towards it, and the medium had to let him pass. Today, I'm sure it was my maternal grandfather. He has since come through in full force, which means that everything is now fine, but that evening we didn't believe it.

Awakening after awakening

As we were about to leave, my mother and I were still sceptical but nonetheless began talking about how as a child I could sense and see people on the family farm that belongs to my father's family. I had seen them in the window and been scared of going into the barn even though I had lived there all my life. My mother went over and asked the medium: 'What if someone can see this, that and the other...?' and already there he turned his gaze on me. He knew perfectly well that it was about me. He explained what I was experiencing and told me to go and pay Marzcia Techau a visit. Her name wasn't familiar to me and I was so full of sensory impressions that I quickly forgot about it again.

But something had been switched on in me, and I took a weekend course with another clairvoyant. During those two days I experienced awakening after awakening, but I only really realised what was going on with me when I facilitated a contact between a deceased father and someone else in the course. She started crying because she was so moved. In fact, it had been quite difficult in the beginning, almost nothing came through. But I have always been very creative and imaginative, so I started inventing things, and she kept saying "yes" to everything I said. When I then suddenly could also say the first name of her father, she broke down completely. I didn't understand how I could know what her father's name was and what he looked like, but I knew I had to continue with this. However, I had the feeling it should be with another teacher, so I searched a bit on the net and found Marzcia's website. I booked an acceptance interview with her, put on my most boring clothes and removed my earrings. I didn't want her to be able to read who I was because I was still testing all this. I come from a family where spirituality was ridiculed; my scepticism therefore ran deep.

Learning to become aware of myself

Before we met, I had expected to see a very serious and solemn lady, but she was smiling with a very light energy. Before we started, she just took the whole living room in hops like a street urchin! But when she began to tell me things, it was as if a veil slipped over her face and she became concentrated. She told me about my childhood, how I had seen the deceased and how I had communicated with my grandmother, who died when I was five or six years old. She could also see what my living room looked like and why I had come. It was quite simply about me needing to learn to become aware of myself: become aware of what I wanted to eat, what I wanted to do and what was my energy. Throughout my life I had been so filled by other people's energies that I couldn't sense my own. Marzcia saw that. She also saw that my biggest fear was aggression. I was so scared that people would get angry or irritated that it almost crackled in the air if I was feeling that way. I always tried to solve the puzzle of whether people in the room were on bad terms. It was all about having my antennae out.

At the end of the conversation, I was told that if I wanted to start one of her trainings, I would be very strong at healing, because I had a healer's heart, but she would still advise me to take the clairvoyance training, because I needed to learn to take care of my sensitivity.

Suddenly not strange

Even though I had neither admitted to her nor to anyone else that I had considered taking her courses, I ended up starting the clairvoyance training.

It was the best decision of my life.

Suddenly I met like-minded people who had had experiences that were similar to mine and who, like me, needed to develop their abilities. We had a common experience of often carrying around other people's feelings; if we had been near someone who was mentally ill or vulnerable, we would have automatically sucked their feelings into us like a sponge to relieve them, and we needed to learn to let go of that. For me, it was more worthwhile to meet someone who had experienced the same thing as I did, than for a psychologist to say, 'I can understand that. How do you experience that?' etc. It is very powerful when you can feel that people believe you without having to apologise for yourself and say, 'I know it sounds crazy.'

The combination of healing and the other people's stories made me start to feel okay and perfectly fine: 'No, it wasn't just my imagination that the pots were falling on the floor or that I saw a man in the window when I was little' – because all the others had also experienced it. The spirit world gave me back a sense of myself. I could straighten my back and say, 'This is how I am.' It had once been the most natural thing in the world. I saw lots of deceased people when I was a child, and I had a language for it. But later I was told over and over again that it wasn't true. My ex-boyfriend even said I shouldn't talk about it if I didn't want be sectioned.

It was also a tough process. I had and still have a tendency to end up in something heavy, so that during the healings, I often went in and grabbed hold of something that made me feel bad for a few days. But when I came up again, I felt better than before and knew I wouldn't end up in the same thing again. I saw it as a clearing-out process where I trained in shutting down for other people and as far as possible only inviting the positive in. And then I was getting to grips with that which is my own, which is from my family and my lineage, the friendships I have had and the environments I have inhabited. I got topics like loneliness or sadness healed, and for every small brick, it got a little bit better.

Recurrence in the lineage

Along the way, it dawned on me how many of my problems recur in my family and my lineage. My niece had a period where she was having a hard time and was lonely at school and I could see that it was the same as her mother and I had been through. My mother has also experienced exactly the same thing – and my grandmother. Four generations have experienced the same thing. Of course, one can say that it is one's social heritage, but that isn't adequate for what these energies can do. I know this because the people I met while I was a social educator had been exposed to their social heritage in a very negative direction. But it isn't the whole story; there has to be something else behind it. I could also feel that my family was healed because I went into this. They would probably still be far from describing themselves as spiritual today, but they are interested in the development it has given us. And I can feel that the healings have also affected some of them, even those who don't believe in it.

As I worked on my spiritual side, I also got in better shape physically. Previously, I had lived off takeaways and cola, for that was all I had the energy to eat. Now I began to be able to eat what my body needed. During the training, I needed lots of protein, eggs and meat, but afterwards I needed plant-based food, not because I have strong political views or am a vegan, it was just about what my body desired.

There were also friendships that ended because of growing apart, as it is called. And I got a new boyfriend who was a completely different type of man than I had had before. I hadn't ever dared to believe that I could feel so good about another human being. I feel so seen, even though he isn't interested in the spirit world. I am accepted and respected for who I am. I don't feel I am a cut-out doll any more; I don't have to wear a mask.

Today will be lovely

The biggest landmark for me was that I woke up one day and thought, 'It's going to be a lovely day – I want to get out of bed.' I can't remember ever having had such a basic joy in having to get up and live my life. To think that it wasn't just something that other people had or that you saw in films – it was actually granted to me too!

I can't work as a social educator any more, working with young people with mental illnesses because I absorb the energy from them. I have therefore started an office-work education. I really like the spiritual aspects of life, the spiritual world is where I belong, but I also need a link to the physical world so that I don't end up like a balloon flying up into the spirit world. Someday I am going to make a living from being a clairvoyant; it is just a matter of time.

I can honestly say that I have turned my life round 180 degrees in the meeting with the spirit world. I eat differently, have dropped my asthma medication, see other people, have another boyfriend and have chosen a new education. It has affected everything from my outlook on life to my trouser size. I have worked with my spiritual aspects, and all sorts of other benefits have come out of that. That wasn't my intention, but it has been heaven-sent!"

***

Endnotes

1   SE stands for Somatic Experience, and the SE education is an education in shock and trauma therapy, which I will say more about in the chapter on trauma and blockages.

2   According to Peter A. Levine in *In An Unspoken Voice*, where he distinguishes between thoughts and consciousness.

CHAPTER 1 – in brief

- A human being consists of four planes: the physical plane (body), the emotional plane, the mental plane (thoughts or beliefs) and the soul plane. The four are mutually regulating and interdependent. If we want both to live in accordance with who we are and feel good, we need to be in balance between the four planes.

- We often over- or under-prioritise one or more planes in our lives and thus get out of balance. We live our lives from our thoughts, are prisoners of our feelings or – less often – are just preoccupied with our bodies. A crisis such as an accident or an illness can force us to restore the balance, but we can also work to do it without anything intense happening first.

- For me, abandoning the very mental activity associated with research within a university environment led to an expansion of another plane, the soul plane or spiritual plane. It has meant that I live today in accordance with who I am and that for which I am here more than I ever would have been able to as a researcher. However, I didn't know this while the crisis was raging, and here I needed the spirit world to help me endure the wait and have confidence that the right thing would happen.

- Just as we operate on four levels, there are also four degrees of readiness for development. The soul is always ready, but the body, the feelings and the thoughts can be ready to varying degrees. When a human being is ready on all four levels at once, development is usually extremely fast.

**AT MARZCIA.DK YOU CAN
FIND THESE MEDITATIONS:**

Pillar of light

Pillar of light charging

Guardian angel express grounding

Angel of Light

Contact your spiritual guides

Healing for today

Liberation from being stuck

CHAPTER 2

THE LIFE OF THE SOUL

About the soul home, (re)incarnation and living
from your soul essence

Mankind's notions of the soul are ancient. We have always known that we were more than our bodies, the thoughts we think and the feelings that arise in our systems. There is an I who transcends all this. What we call this I can vary from one period to another, from culture to culture and from person to person. Within the spirit too, there are different schools, concepts and ways to explain the life of the soul with its connection to the spirit world. My perception of the life of the soul, as I have experienced it in my life, through my studies and through my professional experience, is as follows:

***

Your soul is both your innermost self and a part of the divine, of all the souls in the world. You are completely your own and a part of everything. You are your soul who received a body when you were born as a human being and you live on as a soul when you have finished living in the body you have now. Your soul is thus eternal and without physical limitations. It, and you, are far larger than your physical body. It can be a huge, in fact almost dizzying, realisation, but it is also a huge relief. Not in the way that permits us to be indifferent about our life because there will just be a new one after that, but on the contrary; we live this life as well and meaningfully as we possibly can, without fear and in peace with the knowledge that everything goes on. Life is infinite.

When our souls are not incarnated as humans, animals, or plants here on Earth — or perhaps as beings elsewhere in the universe — they are in a different oscillation or frequency of consciousness that is around us all the time. This is what I call the soul home. The soul home is not a physical place like a house or a country, but a home that is beyond time and place. When the soul is at home, it is connected to all other souls in the soul home; it feels good and is at peace, learning and developing. The souls heal and reflect on the lives they have just lived. They support and help their living and deceased relatives.

Between the spiritual and the physical worlds, there is a dimension where the two worlds meet – I usually call it a pillar of light, but it is not a pillar in the literal sense; it is a dimension between the physical world and the spirit world, like a portal between the two worlds. It is also the tunnel that many with near-death experiences refer to. In this dimension, there is infinite presence, love and light; it is delightful to be here. As a healer, I always connect with this pillar of light when I am going to heal a client. When I do that, I am enveloped by pure love and can share this presence and this love with the client who is also being enveloped. From here, there is unhindered access to the spirit world, the deceased, angels and guides who can offer all the help we need. The sum total of all wisdom, all lived life, is here. We have all been there and we will all be going back there again. And perhaps most important to understand, we all have a part of this divinity in us, for we are both physical and spiritual beings in our earthly lives. We are all in touch with this dimension when we sleep, when we meditate and when we do spiritual work. The spirit world has the possibility of supporting us daily even if we don't consciously make contact, but if we train the contact, we can get more support for both our inner and outer lives.

THE PILLAR OF LIGHT

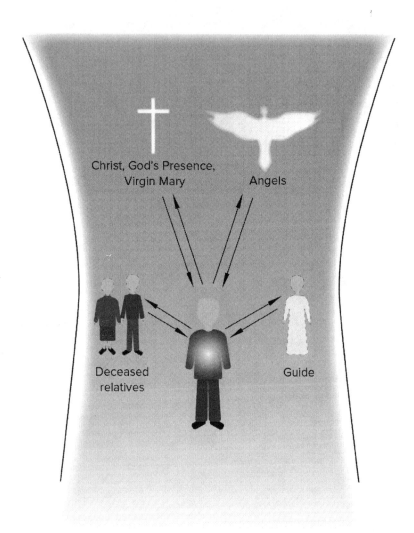

Christ, God's Presence,
Virgin Mary

Angels

Deceased
relatives

Guide

THE SOUL AND THE BODY MEET

When a child is born, there is a strong attraction between a particular soul and the little new body. It isn't like we are "assigned" a body, but rather that there is a meaning that precisely this soul and this body must learn to cooperate. It may be a connection between the purpose of the soul – what it wants to accomplish – and this particular body, or it may be that there are themes that the soul had in previous lives and didn't really resolve, which recur in precisely that body in which the soul lands. This can be quite specific. Several researchers have studied how very young children insistently claim that they are specific people that they shouldn't be able to know at their age. They can point out places and know things that only the deceased person should know. A well-known example is the Swedish author Barbro Karlén (born 1954), who early on claimed that she was the little Jewish girl Anne Frank (1929–1945) who wrote the famous diary. Among other things, Barbro Karlén could find Anne Frank's house in Amsterdam and point out things in the house that only the family knew about. By virtue of the violent life that Anne Frank had lived in the Nazi concentration camp Bergen-Belsen, and not least the violent death she underwent, the Swedish woman also had quite strong life phobias in her current life. I talk about this problem – and how to work with it – in the chapter on karmic healing. The point here is that there is a connection between body and soul which is certainly not random.

The now deceased American psychiatrist Ian Stephenson (1918–2007) did research both into how feelings, mental states and physical characteristics can recur from life to life and into reincarnation being a third factor, in addition to genes and the environment, when it comes to the emergence of conditions and diseases. He showed, among other things, how children could be born with birthmarks that exactly matched, for example, bullet holes or other characteristics of the deceased person that the children said they were – there was a precise and visible match between the soul and the fledgling new body. The same is true of emotional and mental "mother marks," with which, among other things, Stephenson's colleague and later heir, the child psychiatrist Jim Tucker has worked and is still working.[3]

Although soul and body belong together, learning to live together is hard work. When the soul must live in a body, it must descend into a heavier physical vibration and often heavier thoughts, beliefs and negative feelings. The soul and body must learn to cooperate in the life that shall be lived now. It can be a difficult exercise – sometimes the soul can't really adjust to the heavier vibration. For many of us, it becomes a lifelong exercise to process the beliefs or feelings that are causing a blockage, release them and create the space for us to be able to achieve better contact with our soul essence. There may also be periods when part of the soul "slips out" of our bodies. As I wrote in *When The Spirits Come Calling*, I can see it for example in my clients, from the soul being a little crooked in relation to the body or a little displaced. The person is "out in space" and can't really relate to her or his own life. My task will then be to help the person get the soul in place – and give it space. It may sound mystical, but it isn't actually. I am sure you have a lot of everyday experiences that point in that direction. Just think of expressions like "I don't feel comfortable in my body," "I was completely out of myself" or "I feel as if I'm not completely present." They resonate immediately because we have all experienced something like that. Sometimes such an out-of-self-state is due to the fact that we are exposed to something so powerful that we have to "leave ourselves" in order to endure it. In psychology, it is referred to as disassociation if we experience something traumatic such as an accident or an assault. In my view, it is a little bit of the soul essence that slips out until it is possible to be in the body again. The problem arises if we continue to dissociate, even when the danger is over.

However, the challenges of soul-body collaboration don't have to be about trauma; they can also "just" be about you learning to give mental, emotional and physical space to the cooperation with your soul consciousness so that from there you can live your life and function in this world. Your soul doesn't have to be limited by the fact that it now lives in a physical body if you are capable of giving it space. If your soul can be allowed to radiate out through your body, there is plenty of room for it. But if there are too many tensions and blockages, the soul can't be in the body and then some of it slips out again. Or maybe you can't connect with your soul consciousness because it is firmly fixed in physical, mental or emotional blockages. Again, it is important to note that the blockages or tensions don't have to come from this life. They can also come from past lives or from your lineage. Regardless of where it comes from, it is possible to access the soul and give it space, either with the help of a healer, or by connecting yourself to your self-healing potential and the spirit.

It isn't our entire soul that is incarnated every time. The American hypnotherapist Michael Newton (1951–2016) has described in his books on life between lives and the journeys of the soul how it is only a part of a soul that is incarnated to learn something specific. That was one of the things he found out through the regression therapy he developed, in which he led people back to relive not just their childhood lives but the past lives of their souls as well. Part of your soul may thus well be in the soul home – or elsewhere – even if you live here on Earth now. And your deceased family members are still around you, even though their souls may have been incarnated again. For us as human beings it is difficult to understand mentally that the soul is consubstantial with consciousness, mental states and emotional states and moods, not a linear existence like our life here on Earth.

SOUL RETRIEVAL

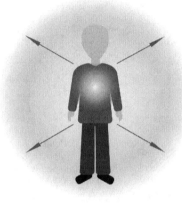

Harmonious and grounded

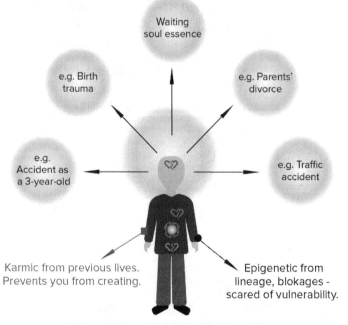

Waiting
soul essence

e.g. Birth
trauma

e.g. Parents'
divorce

e.g.
Accident as
a 3-year-old

e.g. Traffic
accident

Karmic from previous lives.
Prevents you from creating.

Epigenetic from
lineage, blokages -
scared of vulnerability.

Parts of the soul essence need to get
all the way down into the body

SOUL RETRIEVAL – ACCESS

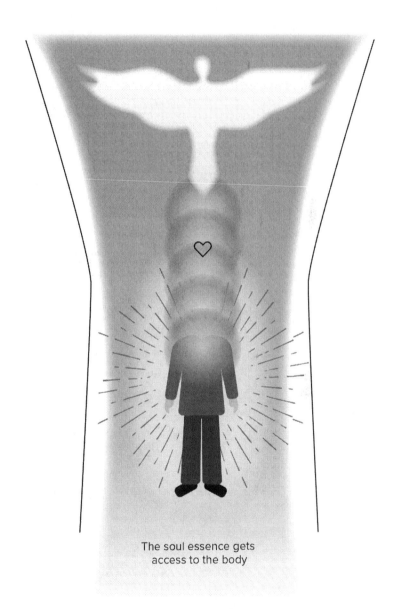

The soul essence gets
access to the body

THE INFINITE CAPACITY OF THE SOUL

The soul doesn't only have traumas and themes from previous lives, but also all of the good it has experienced, the talents and qualities it has immersed itself in. It has feelings, experiences and knowledge – and even physical characteristics and challenges that show up in the body it is living in. I usually say that the soul is the sum of all the incarnations it has had, and they can be human incarnations as well as those of animals, plants or other creatures. The soul is very wise, but access to its wisdom requires that you are ready and that you have a strengthened conscious contact with your soul essence. The soul is fully competent. It has an infinite capacity, but it demands readiness, time and practice to learn to master that capacity and live in accordance with it. You could imagine that the perfect cooperation between your soul and your body is like a beautiful grand piano with an impressive array of keys. When the collaboration works flawlessly, you can play on all the keys – you can play the most beautiful classical pieces of music. Everything is possible! But being able to play all the keys requires both that we, for our part, practise and that the grand piano works. Along the way, some of the keys might get stuck – blockages or trauma – and we can only play all the melodies when we have freed them up. Otherwise, we have to play the tunes that don't contain a C or a D, and that is a limitation.

When the soul is going to live and experience a life on Earth, it is basically full of a desire to experience something in this world and contribute as well as it possibly can. But the heavier physical vibration and the limitations of human life can screen off its luminous consciousness. As I wrote earlier, the soul is always there. If we live in accordance with it, we are better in sync with our life purpose and supported on our path. We make it easier for ourselves by listening to our intuition and by following the path that gives us joy and satisfaction and makes sense to us.

But if instead we live from those parts of ourselves that aren't connected to our soul, then we will identify with those parts. We "become" them. It means we will live from our beliefs: e.g., I have to perform to be allowed to be here; it is expected of me that I do something specific; if I dare to take up space, I will be punished; and so on. The happy, enterprising soul who was so ready to embark on all the good, fun and meaningful things in life will be hidden far away for fear of what will happen if it shows itself as who it is. And then other mechanisms take over – you survive rather than live. Today, for example, many people suffer from anxiety, but as I see it, anxiety is what you have, not what you are. I don't see anxiety as a part of the soul, but as an expression of there being something in you that needs to find peace and become serene. You may of course have a mental illness that makes you very anxious but the illness is still not you, not your soul. Some people talk about tormented souls, but as of yet, I haven't seen a tormented soul in my work. On the other hand, I have seen many tormented people. And it doesn't have to be like that. The more you live in accordance with your soul essence, incarnated and in good collaboration with your feelings, your thoughts and your body, the more intensely present and grounded you become in your life. And then you can live from your deep needs and not from needs that arise in order just to survive.

LIFE BETWEEN LIVES

When earthly life is over, your soul must return to the soul home. Your soul sees the light, turns to it and moves towards it; into the pillar of light and further back into spiritual being. The body dies, but the soul lives on. Many people who have had near-death experiences describe this light and the experience of leaving the body completely. Sometimes, however, something goes wrong in this natural process. For some reason, the soul doesn't turn to the light. It "forgets" to walk towards the pillar of light and come home. Maybe because it is sad about something that has happened in the life it has just lived. It could also be that there is something with which it doesn't feel finished here on Earth. Something of which it can't let go. In my work as a medium, I have even helped many deceased people over into the light so that they were able to come home and, with time, get ready for a new incarnation. I heal both the living and the dead, and as we shall see in the chapters on karmic and epigenetic healing, these areas have enormous potential for healing and development, both for us in this life, for our souls and for our lineage. But if it goes as it should, your soul will come home and feel good and safe until it is time to be incarnated again.

Our souls belong to a soul group, like friends or comrades. It may be that we have been born into the same lineage, but that isn't certain. Your soul friends can, in principle, be anyone at all from the incarnate point of view. You have probably had the experience of meeting people here in earthly life with whom you had an immediate connection, a kind of wordless communication. You know what each other will say before you say it and you feel how each other is feeling, even if you aren't together. It feels like you know each other in a different way than how you know other people.

Your soul can be incarnated countless times. Sometimes there is a long time in the earthly sense between our lives; other times we come back quickly. It can often be the case that if you have suffered a violent death, you will come back again quickly, perhaps to heal the wound inflicted on you last time. All in all, it can be said that for every generation, we try to do the good things that didn't go so well last time, and that we try to take the good things with us to the next life. In this way, we help one another to develop ourselves and thereby develop humanity. In addition to having our soul group, our souls on Earth will often follow the same lineage or the same lineages. Like attracts like, which means that we come down to the same issues, challenges and qualities over and over again. I go into this in depth in the chapters on epigenetic healing and karmic healing.

YOU ARE YOUR SOUL

The most important thing to understand about your soul is that it exists within you. It is no more mystical than that. You already have access to your soul essence, which is divine. And at the same time, there is a world around you of the Presence of God, angels, guides and the dead, where you can get help. All of them are resources on which you can draw. Many people enjoy summoning their guides, getting help from angels, and communicating with their deceased relatives, and they are certainly all ready to help you. But if you only seek help there, you will become dependent on something outside of yourself. That is why it is so important for me to emphasise that if you start living from your soul essence, then you will be connected to something within yourself that has an infinity of resources. You are your soul. Of course, there are all sorts of things that can be tricky in an earthly life. But the state within you is infinite, and when you have peace on the inside, the outside quietly falls into place. Our outer lives reflect our inner lives, just as our inner livese can mirror the outer. With access to your soul, you also have access to your potential, your resources and your team of guides, helpers and spiritual consciousnesses who stand around you and support you – if that is what you want. Your soul is within you, and it is connected with all souls outside of you. You are a beautiful drop in the ocean.

Endnote

3   In the Netflix series Surviving Death (2021), you can follow Jim Tucker's work of visiting and interviewing children who are reincarnations of specific people – and helping their families with this painful realisation.

CHAPTER 2 – in brief

- Your soul is within you and radiates from you and is in contact with the spirit world. The soul has a lighter vibration of consciousness than the physical body. It is infinite and has great capacity.
- Between lives, souls are in the soul home. There is infinite presence, love and light here.
- When a child is born, the soul is incarnated in the small body. There is a strong attraction between soul and body; perhaps the soul has a purpose that suits that body; perhaps there is a theme, talent or trauma that it hasn't finished developing and that suits that body. The soul and the body have to learn to work together, which can be difficult because the body, the feelings and the thoughts create limitations that the soul doesn't have in itself. But it is absolutely possible to learn to give space to the soul so that you can be at ease in the body and radiate into the world.
- The soul carries feelings, proficiencies and experiences with it from life to life. You could say that your soul is the sum of all the incarnations you have had.
- It isn't necessarily your entire soul that is incarnated every time. Part of the soul may well be in the spirit world or elsewhere, even if you are living here on Earth now.
- Between the physical world and the spirit world is the pillar of light – a kind of portal between the two worlds. Souls travel through this when children are born and we die. Angels, guides, and the deceased can freely wander between the soul home and our earthly world to help us.
- When we die, the soul must return to the soul home. It sees the light, turns to it, and goes in that direction. Occasionally it may happen that the soul or parts of it

don't detect the light and therefore don't turn towards it. Then it may need help to get home. This where healing can help.

- You always have access to your soul essence, but it requires you to be ready and aware. When you live in accordance with your soul essence, you have access to all the help and support available in the spirit world. Then your soul can shine out into the world and fulfill its purpose.

**AT MARZCIA.DK YOU CAN
FIND THESE MEDITATIONS:**

Guardian angel, soul light and grounding

Contact your spiritual guides

Your own space

CHAPTER 3

FROM THE PILLAR OF LIGHT TO YOUR LIFE

About healing and your nervous system

The atmosphere is intense. One person is quietly crying while someone else suddenly laughs out loud. A third person has got a nice pink colour in her cheeks, and a fourth sits completely motionless, but her soul consciousness is radiating from her energy field, giving her a feeling of happiness and clarity. There is something going on everywhere; something that unifies us, even if we are not physically together. From the outside it can be hard to see what's going on, but there are truly amazing forces at play, and I know that the development for those who are receiving the healing is profound and life-giving. As always, I am gripped by a deep gratitude for being a part of this healing work, where I make myself available for the loving presence that right now envelops and heals my fellow human beings.

CHANNEL FOR ENERGY

You probably know how it is to come into a room and very quickly, almost instinctively, have a sense of the atmosphere between the people in the room. If there is a nice, loving and inviting atmosphere, you relax and feel safe and open to contact with the others. If it isn't nice, you will respond by looking after yourself, becoming more aware of any dangers and being on your guard. You close off a little to deep contact with the others, keeping your mental and emotional defences up while you wait and see. This often happens completely unconsciously. Your sight and your other senses are in the process of sensing atmospheres and other people. There are parts of our sensory apparatus that are specifically developed for it and which instinctively mirror or resonate with other people. This is partly about your process of adaptation to the group, but it also strengthens the possibility of understanding each other. Susan Hart is a psychologist whose work is mainly about mirror neurons and the importance of spindle neurons in the development of our social, emotional and empathic qualities. In an article in *Psykologi Nyt (Psychology News)*, she writes that biology and psychology meet in the neural pathways, but I would like to add that biology, psychology and soul meet in the neural pathways.

I have been working as a healer since 2001[4] and have in recent years specialised in healing the inner child, karmic healing and epigenetic healing, which I will talk about in later chapters. Basically, however, the same principles underlie all healing. I will therefore take a little space here to explain what healing is to me and why it works the way it does.

MY SOUL'S ABILITY FOR ONENESS

I usually explain it in such a way that, with my highly sensitive nervous system, I feel a bit like a chameleon who instinctively adapts to the atmospheres I am in and the people I am with. This can be both an advantage and a disadvantage. I have thus spent many years teaching myself to be far more aware of where and what my senses are reflecting or are in contact with, both in the physical world and the spirit world. It is precisely this reflectiveness and ability for oneness in my nervous system, along with my soul's ability to be in close contact with the spirit world, that I use as a basis for being a channel for the presence of healing, both in healing myself and when I am the channel for healing other people.

When I heal, I tune my nervous system to a oneness with the healing presence in the spirit world. With my sensory apparatus and mirror neurons, I allow this presence to flow through my entire energy field and onwards to the person who is receiving the healing. The client reflects in her nervous system the presence that surrounds them, and thus begins the healing between the spirit world and the client. It therefore isn't my energy or me as a human being that heals, but the divine healing energy that already exists in the universe. Another extremely important thing about being a healing channel is to set oneself aside, to not disturb or control the healing energy. When I have received teaching from English mediums, the principle has been "More spirit, less you," and this is a core element in all work with the spirit world. The healing energy and wisdom in the spirit world means that it comes with precisely the presence, and creates the possibility for exactly those healing processes and insights, for which the recipient of the healing is ready. In addition, the spirit world has a far greater overview of the world, time, the universe and the context of everything. As a human being, I definitely don't have that knowledge and that overview. I have to acknowledge time and time again, in deep humility and deeply moved, that the most beautiful and incomprehensible processes occur when the spirit world and an individual human being, or a group, meet and the healing can occur.

HOW HEALING WORKS

Healer   Deceased relatives   Guide

WHAT I DO

When I heal, I connect with the pillar of light and come into a state where I am both in close connectedness with the spirit world and in an inner quiet, meditative state within myself. The intention is to be the best possible channel for precisely the healing that my client or course participant needs. Then I enclose the person or people I am healing within the pillar of light so that we are in the same energy field – whether we are 3,000 kilometres apart, online or in the same room. Remember that we are all connected to some degree, emotionally, mentally and on a soul level; whether the client or the course participants are physically present with me in the healing situation is of lesser importance. We step into the non-physical space together, where the spirit world can best connect with us. I connect my sensory apparatus with the spirit world to sense and convey the healing that comes to the client or course participants, but I also pay attention to where the healing wants to help the client, to where he or she has physical, mental or emotional blockages that are ready to be released, or to where in the client the healing wants to support good qualities or states that the person is ready to develop more. Basically, my sensory system communicates the healing from the spirit world, which amplifies the presence around and within my client, the client's sensory system senses the presence, and the healing process gets going. The client gets all the help he or she needs from her own self-healing potential, her own restorative power and from her team of guides, angels or deceased relatives, depending on who it is that can help them best. I always start by inviting everyone in the spirit world who has something positive to contribute to participate; it can be angels, guardian angels, guides, deceased relatives and so on.

HOSTING "THE DINNER PARTY"

When I am the channel for the healing energy, it is that and the spirit consciousnesses that fill me and flow through me to the client. The spirit consciousnesses can also use the common energy field that has arisen to stand around the client and heal him or her. I myself do as little as possible; my task is to maintain the space and the contact between the spirit world, the healing energy and my client. You can think of it as being similar to hosting a dinner party, where your love and your desire for the guests to have a good time and return home enriched are important parts in them feeling safe and starting to exchange thoughts, ideas, love and caring for each other. The guests may have really met each other because of this gathering, soul to soul, and in that meeting may have confirmed both that life is good and that love, solicitude and inspiring people exist: a healing, transforming and rewarding meeting that fills the guests physically, mentally and emotionally. The host has provided the basic setting, but those who meet in that setting have the possibility of much more. In a healing, this meeting takes place between the living in the physical world and the living in the spirit world. As a healer, I see it as my task that my pure inner essence as a flame becomes one with the far greater flame in the spirit world, and that my client's flame also becomes part of the far greater flame. When this happens, the setting for incredible healing between the spirit world and my client is in place, and the point then for me is to follow the path of healing in and around my client.

Through my sensory apparatus, I often become aware of where there is a deficit of energy. I therefore ask for the healing that needs to be provided. When the energy flows in that direction, a development takes place. It gets healed and then I move on somewhere else. The healing energy is constantly enveloping and only where there is a need for extra, do I become extra attentive.

These processes don't always take place consciously. I am drawn to where there is a need, and sometimes I verbalise it if it makes sense. At other times, I just continue without saying anything to the client or student because it will disrupt the process that the person is going through. I often get images or I sense what is being healed in the client. It may be physical things, earlier situations, younger versions of the person and so on. In the same way, I observe what the healing does to my client and who comes to help. That is definitely not all I experience, because my task is to be a channel and maintain the space for the healing to happen. I often get into a very deep, meditative state, where the spirit world has much more access to my sensory apparatus and is thereby much more able to get its healing energy through to my client, so once more: "Less me, more spirit."

ALONE OR IN A GROUP

There isn't much difference between whether I heal a client or I create a healing space around my course participants with the intention of them getting support so that they can learn and get the insights and healing processes they need. When I guide a healing meditation for a group or for my website, my intention is that those who listen receive exactly the healing and insights they are ready for, and for the life and developmental process they are in. However, it is always crucial for me that people know that there is healing present and that they accept it. The intention I have is important for how the healing and the spirit world come through to the recipient. If I am healing several people at once, whether physically or online, I am constantly working with everyone present; they are constantly enveloped and I can feel if some of them should get a little extra support from the healing.

As I heal, I trust that I am sensing what I need to sense, but at the same time I know that I am only sensing the tip of the iceberg. There's a lot going on underneath, much more than I can fathom. A healing session with a client may last an hour, but the healing continues for several hours, weeks or months afterwards, because once the individual begins to open up, it becomes easier for them to be helped, and then it becomes even easier to open up, and suddenly a positive spiral has been created.

YOUR DELICATE NERVOUS SYSTEM

As a biologist and a spiritual person, I am preoccupied with the places where physical human life meets the spirit world, and they really do in healing. The explanation for why it works so well lies not only in the spirit world, but also to a large extent in yourself. There is something you have been doing since you were a baby – completely unconsciously – namely, connecting with your surroundings through your senses and your nervous system. This ability greatly benefits you when you receive healing.

The human nervous system is an amazingly delicate system consisting of nerve cells, nerve fibres, brain and spinal cord. The system's task is to register, process and disseminate information. For example, our nervous system makes it possible for us to feel whether it is cold or hot outside. This information is processed via our sensory nerve fibres into the spinal cord and brain, also called the central nervous system. From here, the information is processed, either completely reflexively by the spinal cord or more intricately and consciously by the brain. Then the information is brought out to the body, which reacts by, for example, contracting the muscles or releasing secretions.

The autonomic nervous system is another nervous system of which we are not masters – we can't control it consciously, hence the word autonomic (independent). This system in turn consists of two opposing nervous systems, the sympathetic and the parasympathetic nervous systems. The sympathetic nervous system controls the adrenal medulla and regulates reactions of anger and fear, making the body "battle-ready"; that is, it increases heart activity, increases the pulse and the blood pressure, pumps blood to the muscles, causes blood sugar to rise and dilates the airways and the pupils. These are all reactions that occur, for example, if you happen to walk out in front of a car or get an unexpectedly tough ticking-off from your boss.

The parasympathetic nervous system promotes the reactions that take place at rest and rebuilds the body; for example, it lowers your pulse and blood pressure, promotes digestion in the gastrointestinal tract, activates the glands, empties your bladder and intestines and causes the pupils to contract. You could also summarise it by saying that the autonomic nervous system is either at rest (parasympathetic) or in battle/flight mode (sympathetic), depending on what we are being exposed to. If there is danger ahead – or if we think there is – we are in the sympathetic nervous system, and if we are safe and calm, we are in the parasympathetic. The ability to regulate our nervous system is crucial to our well-being. If we are in the sympathetic too much, we wear down our body and mind and can develop severe stress reactions or even trauma, and, as we will see in the chapter on trauma, the structure of our brain and nervous system can be both an advantage and a disadvantage for us.

However, in terms of healing and the possibility of receiving help from the spirit world, the structure of our nervous system has a great advantage. There is in fact a clear parallel between how the nervous system connects with the world from the time we are very young and how our soul connects to the presence which it gets access to via healing. As newly born babies, we are completely dependent on the loving presence of our mother, father or other caregivers. Our sensory apparatuses and nervous systems search for this presence and need it, both to survive physically and to come to a state of rest. We can't regulate our nervous system ourselves; we need help from the loving presence of mother or father, stroking our backs, cradling us into their body or softly singing. Later, we learn to regulate our own nervous systems, but we may still need help to calm down.

When I heal, the client or course participants come into a state where the nervous system shifts from the sympathetic to the parasympathetic. The healing conveys a loving presence, an atmosphere, and in the same way that your infant nervous system searched for the presence of your mother or father when you were little, your adult nervous system now searches for the emotional nourishment, deep peace and repose that healing offers. At the same time, your soul is used to connecting with other souls – it knows them "from home," from the soul home, as I described in the previous chapter – the presence from the spirit world that healing offers is therefore a win-win on all four planes.

IN CONTACT WITH THE SENSORY SYSTEM

If my students are not used to registering presence, they will first have to get in touch with their sensory system, which senses the state of their body; this can be associated with discomfort, because the body stores all the feelings you have had throughout your life, including the bad ones, but it also stores the intense experience it can be to be alive. If you opt out of being in touch with your bodily sensations, you also opt out of a very large part of being alive and enjoying taking life in. That is why I often start by helping people into better contact with bodily sensations and to start letting go of what is locked and tense. I put it this way; you are not your feelings, your thoughts or your physical form – you are you, but who is that? What would you be like if you had the possibility of being yourself without restrictions? If you had had all the conditions around you that you needed, who would you then have become? I ask the client or students, while they are in the relaxed state, to let go and receive where there is space to do so. The healing presence gives them access to their soul essence, the relaxed presence, and they begin to sense that they can feel safe. They get in touch with a place in themselves where it is nice to be: a place with inner peace without blockages and tensions. There are no chaotic thoughts or feelings here, and there are no physical tensions. The individual can feel who he or she is in this space and can begin to listen to his or her own inner voice. For some people, it is unusual to be in such a space – they may even be a little scared of being in a place where it is okay to enjoy oneself without having to give something in return, in a state of being without doing. We often think we need to be something to have a raison d'être. We keep ourselves on a short leash and scold ourselves if we just happen to be enjoying ourselves. But when you come down to the essence of the soul and experience that you have a raison d'être without having to perform, and that your very being in itself has permission to be here, then you can radiate from there. For some people, it will be too overwhelming to listen inwardly, especially if they have never done so before. In that case, they can listen to the presence outside instead. They can connect with the pillar of light and contact the spirit world in the form of angels, guides, and dead relatives. These are always ready to help, even though it may be too intense for you to look inwards. During the healing, there is space and calm to relax completely and, in that situation, it may well be that the body begins to react and twitch; you may start quivering and feel heat due to increased blood flow in muscles which were tense before. It happens because something that has been in a locked state can now begin to complete the movement previously blocked by shutdown from the traumatic event. The reaction is reminiscent of the way wild animals recover from being attacked – the impala shaking off an attack from the lion or the rabbit that goes completely stiff and plays dead when the fox is close by, only to subsequently come out of its frozen state, shake itself and hop away as we will see in the chapter on trauma and blockages. In this state, some people may also become sad because feeling the help and support can evoke memories of the times when it wasn't there. You could say that when the light breaks through, it also shines where it is dark. While it may be hard, it is totally okay to get in touch with these sad feelings. We often break down when we are met with what we have been missing.

I experienced this myself when I was little and my cat died. I had an important person in my life who I felt was like my big sister. When she met me with loving attention after I had lost the cat, I completely broke down because that was where it was possible. The bubble burst and I was able to process an emotional part of the grief. Usually, I was such a little squirt with a lot of get-up-and-go, but when I was with her, I got more in contact with my vulnerability. At home, there was a lot of emotional turmoil and my parents were very busy. With the vulnerability I have brought with me, I had to barricade myself to be able to be in that chaos. When I then met the presence and attention of my "sister," my defences broke down and that was a good thing, because then I was released. In the same way, during healing, some people may experience that their defences are broken down, and the healing rebuilds what needs to recover and what needs to have space to grow.

WHEN MY ANKLES MISFIRED

Healing is about surrendering to the help that is found around us and within ourselves all the time. An experience from my own life shows how this is something at which we can steadily improve. On 14 October 2020, after a short period of calm after the first corona lockdown in Denmark, I had a very intense healing meditation. The theme was getting more of my soul essence connected to my body and the life I am living here on Earth. It was a powerful meditation where both my ankles, on which I don't usually have much focus, started to get very hot and radiate like little suns. I got so much flow through my body and the feeling of standing strong and good in my life, radiating out into the world and helping to create more light, love and insight, was so profound that the spirit world was better able to manifest itself.

Six hours later, as I was going down the stairs from my students on the first floor, I twisted my left ankle. The ankle buckled completely, and when the right one had to take the weight, I twisted that one too. It all happened very slowly, and as it was the last step on the stairs, there was no shock or twitching in my body, no drama at all. But I had two very strained ligaments in my left ankle, and my right ankle was fractured in several places. I managed to get up, but my ankles weren't working; there was no contact to my feet. Twelve training people on which the students were going to practise had arrived, and I sent them up to the students. I then manoeuvred myself over to the sofa, from which I couldn't get up again. My body was shaking and there was nothing to be done. I now tried to ring up to my students, but they had switched off their phones, and so had Jette. I thus waited until the students had finished, and gave them the last hour of teaching from the sofa when they came down. If I lied completely still, there was no pain; it was therefore just a matter of staying calm. It was only later that I got hold of Jette, who contacted the emergency medical service, and I got transported to the hospital.

It became clear at the hospital that I would have to have surgery on my right ankle, and that both legs had to have total peace. The eight days I was hospitalised was one big healing process, not just physically, but perhaps especially mentally, emotionally and in my soul. I have always had a very energetic and mobile, strong body and a large number of balls in the air and projects going on at the same time. Suddenly that was all gone. On the other hand, I was greeted by overwhelming warmth, healing and care from my surroundings. It was while corona was at its peak, which meant that only Jette could visit me, but the contact with people via Facebook and my networks was intensely transforming.

I have been very giving in my life but haven't been so good at expressing when I needed help or care, just as I haven't been good at accepting when help or care was offered. Now I was lying here and couldn't do anything else but surrender. And it worked! Love, flowers and sincere warm-heartedness poured into me. The feeling deep down that I am loved and valued, and that I no longer needed to be on my guard and could just receive, was overwhelming and transformative. I am very grateful to all those who supported and helped me during that period.

During those days, I got healing from many healers and received so much healing support for the inner and outer processes that were going on. Colleagues, students, friends, family and acquaintances, even people with whom I hadn't had contact in years contacted me with a hello or a caring message. Help was offered. It was as if a wall inside me had been knocked down and, maybe for the first time in my life, I could begin to feel that I belong here on Earth, and that I am loved and valued and that I can allow myself to receive and be filled. I had a sense of being entitled to be here, not only for what I do, but also for the person I am. I gained a much deeper acceptance of this, also emotionally. It was almost a rebirth process where more of me and my soul essence could find space. I experienced exactly what I have written here: that security, love and feeling loved provide space and peace in the nervous system and the body so that the soul can fill and strengthen its collaboration with the body and the physical life.

Throughout the process, I had a minimal pain, but I was in contact with many traumas, shocks, and injuries from earlier in my current life and from past lives that I hadn't worked on enough, and I clearly felt the help of the spirit world, my deceased relatives and animal friends. Every night an intense healing process. For example, right at the beginning of the hospitalisation, I had contact with a lot of healing guides who were standing around my right foot. Some of them were high consciousnesses, who were reminiscent of elves. I had a clear feeling that they came from Fælledparken, the largest park in Copenhagen right next to the Rigshospital, and that part of their task was usually to heal patients at the hospital. I was very grateful for that experience. It was so nice in my ward, which was filled with flowers and healing presence from both the spirit world and the people with whom I was in contact.

Of course, I was in pain right after surgery, and here I used my access to the pillar of light and my soul essence to bring calm to my body and my pain. There is a lot of research which shows that meditation reduces pain, and here I both meditated and healed at the same time, while connected to my soul. I was overwhelmed by the difference I experienced between being trapped in the physical pain and lovingly accepting and meeting it from my soul and the flow of healing. I plan to investigate this method further to see if it can help other people who are in pain too.

During the hospitalisation, I also had the experience of being able to handle twenty-six hours of fasting while waiting for my surgery, which was constantly being postponed. I can't usually manage without food for four or five hours before my blood sugar drops and I begin to feel really bad, both physically and mentally. But this time, there were no problems. I see this as a result of being supported by healing – my system took in energy from outside rather than eating into my own reserves. After twenty-six hours, I was finally allowed to eat for two hours before I had to fast again and be ready for surgery the next day. The next day, the nicest, most talented team was ready for me, and I had a very good experience: no inconvenience from the anaesthesia, and it took only two and a half hours from the time I was moved from the ward to when I came to the surface again. What a process!

A little extra anecdote is that, after not being able to be of any great use at home for three months, I thought that I had now become so good at walking with crutches and the support of my "ski-boot" bandage on the broken ankle that I could easily help with the hoovering. I therefore grabbed the cord of the kitchen machine to take the plug out of the socket, but after weeks on crutches, the strength in my arms had become a little more than usual, and I suddenly found myself with the whole socket in my hand. I had simply pulled it out of the wall. It was also the most used socket in our home and, on top of that, of course, this happened on a Saturday. The electrician had to go and fetch some extra-long screws so that the rawlplug could get an extra good purchase. I perceived the incident as a clear message that I needed to spend a little more time calmly and patiently recovering, but that I was gaining more strength and building a stronger foothold from which to master the force that was on the way. However, one of my Healing for the Day subscribers thought it was probably a bit too early to start hoovering.

ONENESS AND PEACE

I don't see healing as an energy flow, but as a way to help the one being healed to access different emotional states and states of consciousness within themselves by being met with tenderness and gentleness. In the same way that we feel that we are standing on the ground, listening and watching, our nervous systems respond to the atmospheres and presence that come from the spirit world. You could say that healing uses your deeply inherited instinctive ability to search out loving presence and positive atmospheres for your healing process. You will enjoy the warmth and support that is in the spirit world and can now begin to let go of what is causing blockages. And your soul, which is accustomed to connecting with other souls, connects almost telepathically and in deep presence with the other souls in the spirit world, gaining space and fullness in your life. Through the healing work, we can create a connection to a deep, peaceful space in our innermost being. The ability of our souls, bodies, thoughts and feelings for self-healing will be supported and activated. And then our innermost soul essence can begin to heal and seek contact with the spirit dimension, where there is a deep recognisability of oneness. This is development.

All of this is probably happening without you being aware of it. Your nervous system works very unconsciously and the soul essence is also to a large extent unconscious. The fact that a safe presence is created sets a healing process in train so that there is space to live and be safe within yourself. You become strengthened and recharged. You experience an openness and readiness for life. The body is accustomed to living with an eye open for the next danger, but when you enter the pillar of light during healing, the soul knows perfectly well that there is no danger; we live and die, and we come back again – we are infinite. When we have access to the soul essence, we know that even though the physical body dies, everything else continues, and there is peace with all that exists in this moment. It is difficult for us because, as human beings, we want a focus and a goal, but it is also often right there that we close off; that we put limits on our way of being. Because if we just rush off wilfully, it is often at that point that we shut off for all the splendid help that exists. When you have reserves of energy and a sense of being supported and helped, you engage with life in a completely different way. There will be a different base, and that's very much what we work with, both in healing and in the work of creating a spiritual personal development process.

SMALL STEPS

You can start by having an awareness of how you find peace. Do you make the time and space in your life to just be you, not having to perform, but just being and enjoying? A space where you can be in touch with yourself and your own energy without using it? Some experience that state of mind when doing something creative. If you are a creative person, it may come to you when you are drawing, when you are working with clay, or when you are sewing; you step into a place where time and space don't exist and the world outside disappears. You are absorbed and an inner peace arises. You don't need to think about spirits or angels, you can just immerse yourself in your painting or your knitting without having to do anything else. If you are a very physical person, it may be that you get into that state when you are out running without thinking about anything else except putting one foot in front of the other and feeling the pounding of your heart, the wind in your hair and the freedom. Or when you are out walking, swimming or exercising with no other goal than it being nice for your body to work and the brain being able to find calm. For me, cooking and eating is almost a meditation. When I stand slicing vegetables, or when I eat a well-prepared meal, I get an inner attention, a calmness and a well-being that opens up my presence. I get in touch with myself completely without having to connect with the pillar of light or call on my guardian angel or anything else exalted. You don't have to consciously connect to the spirit world, but you can certainly begin by becoming more aware of what creates the peace in you that lets you come into contact with your soul essence. When you do that, you can always have that state with you, even without having to sew or run or cook. Many of us tend to opt out of the things in life that give us energy, inner peace and oneness because something else (or someone else) is shouting louder and demanding our attention. But when we take the time to fill ourselves with the state of being in touch with ourselves, it gives us access to live our lives from a more authentic place. Music can do something of the same; if you love music, you can always get in touch with that state within you just by hearing a few notes. Instead of sitting with your hands clutched around the steering wheel on the way home, you can sit listening to music and let it be the time when you recharge so that you can be there for your family.

Making room for that space within yourself allows something new to grow within you, and that is healing in itself. These are tiny adjustments that you may know from mindfulness meditation – reaching inside to the best place where we come in contact with our innermost essence. In there, there is calm, ideas and inspiration. In essence, this is what healing is all about: when we create an inner or outer space of calm, help comes.

SELF-HEALING

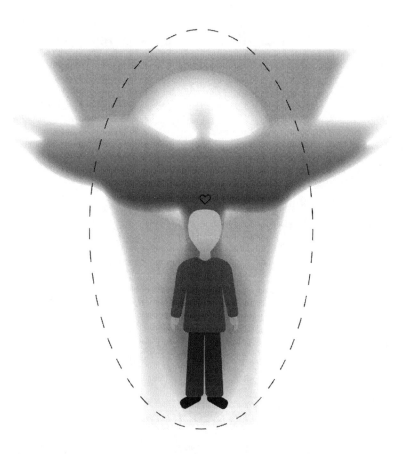

If you are ready for the next step, you can also do a little spiritual practice. I myself began many years ago in this way: sit down in the morning with the intention of contacting the pillar of light, the dimension between the physical world and the spirit world. Allow yourself to imagine that you are surrounded by a loving, safe presence. Maybe you experience it as a luminous presence. Your soul recognises the presence, and your system begins to relax all by itself. Now you can ask for help for the day; it can be from God, the angels, guides or just the healing presence. In this way, you get healing and support for the day, and you get to have the feeling of being in place in yourself before you rush off to work or into your thoughts, and the worries and the to-do list take control of your life. You stay in touch with your inner self and have an easier time engaging with life. Do the same in the evening. Pray for healing so that whatever may be revolving in your mind can resolve itself, and you have peace to let go of the day and surrender to sleep and the night. Notice how just getting in touch with yourself also puts you in touch with something bigger. Totally without the use of a healer, you can thus open yourself to both healing and guidance from the spirit world.

I believe that we humans are here on Earth to experience something for ourselves and to disseminate or give something to the world. If we don't make room for what we are deep down, it is difficult to fulfill some parts of our original purpose in being born on Earth. As a healer, of course, I want to be available as a channel, but in reality, I would wish to be unemployed. Because that would mean that people had learnt to open themselves to their soul-consciousness and the support that is always present from the spirit world.

Endnote

4   There is more about my path into healing in my book *Når ånderne banker på* (*When the Spirits Come Calling* – but this unfortunately not available in English).

CHAPTER 3 – in brief

- Healing is about connecting with the presence, the infinite support and love that is in the spirit world. This energy is always present in the universe; you can connect with it yourself, or a professional healer can help facilitate the contact to it.

- As infants, we are used to orientating ourselves towards a loving presence from our parents or other caregivers by using our senses and our nervous systems. We are in fact completely dependent on it, because we can't adjust ourselves into a calm state yet. This searching within the surroundings and reflection of the presence is what happens in healing, where our nervous system searches for the calm, loving presence from the universe and reflects it in our interior. The more you open yourself to the loving presence, the more you come in contact with your own soul essence, and the more oneness you feel with your soul.

- Your soul helps a lot in the process; it is used to connecting with other souls, so that when you give space to that part of you, you get even more help, and when you get help, there is even more development of yourself and your resources – it is a positive feedback system.

- You can begin to heal yourself by giving space in your life to a place where you are just you and don't have to perform; it can be, for example, through creative pursuits, physical training, listening to music or other experiences where you come into a state of peace and flow and are completely yourself.

**AT MARZCIA.DK YOU CAN
FIND THESE MEDITATIONS:**

Healing for today

Let go of today

Healing of a future situation

Pillar of light recharging

Contact your spiritual guides

CHAPTER 4

TRAUMA AND BLOCKAGES LIMIT YOU

About trauma work and the supportive power of healing
When we don't have proper contact with our soul essence and thereby exclude the possibility of living as who we are, it is quite often because we have traumas and blockages in our system, either from experiences or influences in this life, in previous lives (karmic) or in our lineage (epigenetic). It is as if something is standing in the way and locking us off from the possibility of there being space for us as we are. Healing supports and helps the individual to loosen up the traumas and blockages, so that the energy can flow freely again and there is plenty of room for connectedness with our soul.

***

In 2018, I started training as an SE (Somatic Experiencing) therapist. The Somatic Experiencing® method was developed by the American biophysicist and psychologist Peter A. Levine (born 1942). The method is groundbreaking in shock and trauma therapy and works on how our nervous system cooperates with our beliefs, feelings and bodies.

In addition to Peter A. Levine's understanding of the importance of the nervous system, one of the most important things in the SE method is supporting the client in gaining contact with their internal or external resources because when a client has enough strength to process the trauma, their nervous system, feelings, thoughts and body will be able to be restored. Another important thing is to be very gentle and proceed very slowly.

A trauma is an overload of shocking or stressful situations and arises because something has gone too fast or has been too intense for the client to process. The client therefore feels threatened and the body is still on alert even if the client has come out of the stressful situation. SE is a slow and gentle working method, which allows the client's system to process the experience gradually and assemble more energy resources to heal.

Nowadays, I combine what I have learnt in SE about trauma work with healing and help from the spirit world. In addition, I have found inspiration in Bruce Lipton's theories about the intelligence of cells, which in short means that the environment around the cells is crucial for which genes are activated in the DNA. In relation to healing, this will mean that a loving presence from the healing creates an environment of security, to which the cell membrane responds, and there will be signals to activate genes which tell us that it is nice and safe where we are. Another fascinating thing is the gene activations we have inherited from our lineage, but I will go into this in more detail in the chapter on epigenetic healing. I am thus drawing on knowledge from psychology and biology as well as from the spirit world when I support people in getting rid of their blockages and traumas and living a life in harmony with themselves.

A trauma is an injury to our body or mind as a result of an incident or experience. Many people think of war when they hear the word trauma, but trauma can also arise from serious accidents or very negative emotional experiences. However, not all unpleasant experiences are traumatic; something extra is required. You could say that trauma occurs when our limit of what we can handle is exceeded. In reality, a trauma occurs after a form of fracture, whether it is of our thoughts, our feelings, or our body. To protect what is "fractured," the trauma now closes around that which is vulnerable in us. The trauma takes care of us by closing around that particular part of us. It actually makes sense. The problem is that, by being cut off from parts of ourselves, we have limited access to our resources. Even though the trauma protects us, it also limits us until one day, through therapy and/or healing, for example, we release it and restore ourselves.

WHY DOESN'T THE IMPALA GET TRAUMATISED?

Peter A. Levine has a fundamentally physical and psychological approach to trauma; instead of talking to a traumatised client about what has happened, as in classical therapy, and trying to change the thought patterns and thereby release the trauma in the body, he goes in via the client's bodily sensations and the nervous system's ability to restore calm. Often with help of slow physical movements, he gently gets the client to regain her or his strength to process the trauma physically, emotionally and mentally. When the body feels helped to find its own healing potential, it continues the process of self-healing. This can be done with physical movements, crying, anger or other reactions that are given permission to be expressed in the present. The client is thereby released from the locked state caused by the trauma. One of the important principles is that, as a therapist, you don't go directly into the trauma, but start quietly around it: how was it before the traumatic event occurred? When did you first feel safe after the experience? And then quietly approach the trauma itself. I also have that practice as a healer – tenderness and gentleness are important!

Peter A. Levine has developed his methods partly on the basis of studies of wild animals. In nature, animals are exposed to violent and potentially life-threatening events all the time – small animals are in danger of being eaten by medium-sized animals, medium-sized animals are hunted by large animals and so on. There are attacks, escapes, injuries and near-death experiences in the air every single day. Yet one doesn't see the animals in nature being traumatised in the same way that we humans are. On the contrary, we see the impala grazing calmly on the savannah, relatively soon after they have literally been aggressively hunted by the lions. They don't look like an animal in shock over almost becoming lion food! One of Levine's most important observations is that after a violent experience, the animals shake themselves back; that is, quite literally shaking their body and, in that way, getting their system back into a normal and calm state. It is a reaction where the animal releases the accumulated energy that the sympathetic nervous system has set in motion, via adrenaline among other things, so that the muscles can relax and the parasympathetic nervous system begins to be able to take over. We humans have this ability too, but unfortunately, we also have the ability to suppress it. The tension in the muscles, the "locked sympathetic stress response," therefore remains in our bodies so that parts of us are still in a survival state for a long time after the experience and can't relax.

RUNNING FROM THE LION

When we as humans are faced with a dangerous situation – whether it is a car driving through a red light and coming close to hitting us, or a choleric boss reprimanding us forcefully – we orientate ourselves with our senses: turn our head a little, looking for the danger, and then our brains quickly lay out a plan for us, just as the impala will make a plan to escape the lion that suddenly springs out with wide open jaws. For example, the brain plans for us to run as fast as we can from the car or the boss (which in the case of the impala is similar to the lion). However, this plan can be thwarted. The impala may be caught by the lion, we may not be able to get away before the car hits us, or we will remain standing in front of the boss because we dare not do anything else for fear of losing our jobs. It may be that we go into fight mode, but when that doesn't succeed either, because we are up against too superior a force, we freeze. In the wild, it can save an animal's life because the predator doesn't activate its hunting instinct when the prey doesn't run away, or through its instincts leaves the "dead" animal alone so as not to eat a diseased animal and become ill. For us humans, going into a freeze state can also save us, either immediately – we refrain from pummelling or running from the boss and thereby don't lose our jobs – or delayed; we leave ourselves in the situation, shut down a bit or dissociate so that the verbal abuse doesn't feel quite as bad. Thus far, there is actually not much difference between us and the animals. The tricky part happens when we have been prevented from fighting or fleeing in this way, but the plan to fight or flee continues within us. If we were an impala on the savannah, we would either be eaten by the lion – and then it would be over this time around – or we would shake our bodies thoroughly and calm down again, ready to continue grazing. The shaking would simply restart our system, which would release the accumulated frozen energy. But as humans, we are different from animals in being controlled by the part of the brain called the neocortex. It sits in the cerebral cortex and controls our actions and planning. Instead of running far away from the boss who is standing shouting at us, giving her a slap or shaking her reprimand well and truly off ourselves, the neocortex makes us stand still, listen to the reprimand and maybe even gives the boss a little credit in her unreasonableness for the sake of a good atmosphere in the future, even if her shouting exceeds what we can actually bear to hear.

On the one hand, having a neocortex is a great privilege. Through it, we have the ability to plan and reflect on our own existence. In the actual situation, it is also good that we don't physically start fighting a battle with our angry boss. On the whole, it is good that the neocortex controls our impulses, because it enables a human and compassionate existence where we don't run around beating each other up (all the time). But

84

in relation to trauma, the neocortex has made us vulnerable, because it indirectly prevents us from shaking the violent experience off and calming down like the animals do. The original plan to flee or fight, which you overruled using your neocortex, continues to run inside you, even though the situation is over. This means that you don't come into such good contact with your parasympathetic nervous system again, but instead continue in the sympathetic alarm nervous system. Without thinking about it, you are perhaps exposing yourself to the same situation time and time again to unconsciously try to live out the plan, or perhaps you have to lock yourself mentally, emotionally or physically and cut yourself off from parts of yourself. Your system goes into partial freeze mode so that you can move on. That is our survival strategy. The freeze mode is not a relaxed mode but a stiff "in high alarm" mode. Instead of calming down again when the "lion" has gone and you have survived, you continue rushing to and fro, and that not only means that you are stressed – which is bad enough in itself – but also that it will be difficult or perhaps impossible for you to live in harmony with yourself. For it is in relaxation that there is room for you to live in accordance with your soul essence. If you stay in your system's experience of being in danger, and the alarm response is thus activated within you – whether it is about driving a car, making a career or inner beliefs that you need to achieve a lot – then you will eventually be pushed away from a deep, inner peace where you have access to other levels of consciousness. Then you are trapped in patterns that aren't good for you.

INTERNAL SHIPPING CONTAINERS

When we live with many unprocessed traumas or partially frozen states, we restrict our thoughts, bodies and feelings and therefore also our access to our soul essences. As I wrote in the first chapter, the four planes – body, feelings, thoughts and soul – influence each other; a blockage on one plane is related to blockages on the other planes. Once you have been subjected to an overwhelming state, mentally, physically or emotionally, the muscles still envelop the state, even though in reality it is over. The muscle is still receiving input from the sympathetic nervous system that there is danger; it is tense and ready to either hit out or flee; you therefore can't relax and start processing the state. You have limited access to your resources, which are locked in, and you use your energy to keep the place locked until there are either enough resources to process the state, or your system becomes so frayed that it breaks down.

It sounds inappropriate, but there are good reasons why we function that way. If something is too overwhelming to process or heal at once, our systems, which are designed for survival, will find ways to move forward without processing it. For example, if you have had a broken arm, then the arm grows back together, but the feelings it triggered when it broke – the fright associated with the injury – may lie repressed as locked areas or tensions in your nervous system. It may mean that you get some beliefs and thoughts about yourself and life, which are based on the unpleasant experience. You may lose faith in your ability to seize life and succeed. Perhaps you have a feeling of losing your grip – that is, beliefs that actually originate from the fracture of the arm, but have now become mentally and emotionally locked areas in you. All of this is normal and something we all come across to some degree. Throughout our lives, we all have different experiences that leave their mark on us; some of them restrict us, others strengthen us. And it isn't always possible for us to fully discern where the individual belief or imprint comes from. As we become more aware of why we act, think and feel as we do, we can begin to weed out what is causing blockages in us.

In order to learn how to work with your blockages, it is important to understand that the blockages you have often hold an opportunity for personal growth in one way or another, even though you may not see it until afterwards. As I said, the blockages hold back that with which you aren't ready to work. They have served you well but it comes to a point where they aren't useful any more. I usually compare it to the muscles being like shipping containers, which are securely locked until it is time to open them. They can be stacked and packed, but it takes space and resources to keep them closed and stored out of the way. This means that your system spends a lot of energy on repressing and keeping old feelings and experiences at bay in order to move forward in life. In short: you are shutting down more and more parts of yourself, and your life energy is being used to control what is allowed to come to the surface. It is being used to survive, not live. If you accept that there are a lot of stacked containers, non-flow and physical stagnation, which are associated with stagnation in your feelings or thoughts, and do nothing about them you may eventually experience problems. The body wants to live, and the feelings want to enjoy and live and experience, to create love, be in connectedness, and they can't do that so well if there are blockages. So if you create an access to the body, you will also have access to the locked areas in the feelings and to the thoughts creating the bad habits and patterns. In other words: what is keeping you locked?

CONNECTING WITH A LOVING PRESENCE

In SE therapy, the work is with letting the client get more in touch with the ability to navigate in both the inner and the outer world. The trauma work takes place in a gentle, loving setting so that the body, the feelings and the thoughts can heal themselves and arrive at a peaceful place. It may be that the body is physically quivering and jerking to release the accumulated energy and possibly completing the movements it wasn't given the opportunity to implement in the situation, and it may be that feelings of anger or tears emerge. I combine knowledge from SE with healing and the help of the spirit world that I described in the previous chapter. The healing in collaboration with the trauma therapy sets in motion a positive feedback mechanism: when the nervous system calms down and the body relaxes, the feelings, thoughts and soul get more space. The reverse is also true: when there is space for the soul essence, the nervous system becomes calm. The healing comes in a bit like music that makes a very fine contact with the unconscious parts of you and your sensory apparatus. It causes your autonomic nervous system to feel a pleasant atmosphere and begin to heal because it feels safe (the parasympathetic system). Perhaps you aren't mentally prepared, but the body tells you that it is okay, that it is actually beginning to feel safe. When your body begins to report that it is safe, your feelings may begin to relax, and then your thoughts may also relax. It may also be that your feelings relax first and pull the other planes along with them. Regardless of the order, the nervous system will begin to respond and lead you to a better place. This is what healing can do because it takes advantage of the fact that all the way back from childhood we have been used to regulating our nervous systems according to our parents and surroundings. These are some very basic things in our human nature that healing supports so that we can be repaired from scratch without the disruptive control of the neocortex. Only when we are ready to move on from there can we get deeper relief that sits in the connective tissue and in the nervous system. In this way, one can say that where a psychologist goes from the brain and the mental plane out into the body, then healing can actually go the opposite way, from the body plane via the feelings to the mental plane.

TRAUMA CAN MAKE YOU STRONG

Working with mental, emotional or physical trauma can be hard. No matter how gently it is done, you revisit your trauma, and when you feel that there is a supportive and loving presence, you also sense – again – where it has been missing earlier. It may be hard work, but it is good work. Some of my clients feel that if they go in and feel the pain, they can feel that they are alive. They experience a great relief from getting past the pain, meeting themselves and being able to receive love. That is how it is for all of us. While it might be nice to avoid it, we won't move on if we don't look at what prevents us from being who we really are. And that may be harder than it sounds. Sometimes you just have to do a half-turn to find the sunshine, other times you have to go through a closed door. Whether it is the one or the other is about what kind of theme you are facing. Is it about the fear of letting go or the fear of taking hold? You need to have confidence that your body remembers everything, your feelings remember everything, your soul has every opportunity in the world to heal, and you have all the help you need when you are ready. Then, when you work with your traumas, for example, with the help of a therapist and/or a healer, there is often an extra gain in the form of increased inner strength when you release and move on. Because when the healing goes in and adds exactly the resources that are needed for you to process or digest your trauma, it often happens that your capacity isn't only regained, but even expanded. This is because you have just had an experience of coming through something that previously blocked you, and you have been equipped to be able to handle a similar load again. In addition, you have gained access to more of your soul potential. The healing process thus itself creates new insights and thereby a new security. If, on the other hand, you are still afraid that the same thing will happen again, it is an indication that your trauma hasn't been fully processed. Then there will always be something that will take you back and activate the discomfort that is attached to the trauma or the experience you have had – you are still "running away from the lion" or almost "back in the lion's jaws." When we have such an unprocessed trauma, we try our best to avoid the unpleasantness while simultaneously being pulled in exactly the direction we don't want to go – just to go through what we are trying to avoid. Perhaps you yourself have some experiences in your baggage where you think "Why can't I just walk away from it? Why can't I forget it?" But the trauma is a part of you, it has cut you off from a part of your capacity, and therefore there is no way around working with it.

For example, if you burned yourself on a wood-burning stove as a child, and it really hurt, you can get help to process the trauma; your wound heals, and you are told by your mother and father that you shouldn't just slap your hand on the oven, but grasp the cool handle instead. That way, the experience becomes a moment of learning, because now you can master something you didn't master before, and what was an unpleasant experience actually becomes a strength. But if you don't get your trauma worked out, and no one explains to you what happened or what you could have done differently, then the experience may remain in you as a fear of wood-burning stoves, as a feeling of sadness and fright and a conviction that you shouldn't go near wood-burning stoves again. If we work on the trauma in a good way, we can actually get something even better out of it than what we came from. We can learn to master that situation in such a way that we get the most out of it. By quietly and calmly resolving the trauma, you have the best possibility of using yourself again, now with an even greater wisdom about what the traumatic experience could teach you.

THE WIDE RIVER OF LIFE

None of us get through life without blockages or trauma. Peter A. Levine operates with a beautiful concept, which he calls the river of life. There are some times in our lives when the river is very narrow because we have too many traumas. We use a very small part of our capacity. When we then get our traumas healed, the river becomes wide again, we have greater capacity, the water flows calmly on its way, and we don't end up so easily on the bank where we go into a frozen state or resignation, or over on the other bank where there is fight and flight. The more we stay on the wide river, the more peace, broad-mindedness and robustness we have, and that is what I work with as a healer. The broad-mindedness is not about going along with ideals you fundamentally disagree with, but about building up a capacity not to let other people's weird ideals gain access to your system. Instead of taking those in or letting others overwhelm you, you remain centred in yourself with love and warmth and let others be who they are. This requires you to be in control of both your conscious and your unconscious responses. You need to know your nervous system, your thoughts and your feelings to be able to handle having a wide river. But it is possible and the ability already lies in your soul.

***

Sarah's story:
'I HAVE LEARNT TO LISTEN TO MYSELF – AND I HAVE BEEN GIVEN THE TOOLS TO DO SO'

Thirteen years ago, when Sarah was 48 years old and working as a specialist lawyer, and busy with family, friends and personal interests, she was in an accident that tore her everyday life down in an instant. Through healing, hard work and support from the spirit world, she has gained a life where she no longer throws herself into everything – but has time and energy for her grandchildren and for travelling.

"The accident happens one day when I am out with a friend to buy a horse. When we get out there, my friend doesn't want to get on the horse and, bold as I am, I say I will do it. Since I myself once bought a horse at the place, I actually have trust in them, but when I see that the reins are attached to the noseband, there is something that tells me that I should let them stay there. This feeling turns out to be true, because the horse had been broken in roughly and had its mouth tugged at a lot. However, no one tells me all this, and I go with my brain, which says that the reins should be down in the bit. I don't listen to my intuition.

While I am sitting on the horse, I can feel that I shouldn't touch the reins, and I am a good rider, so I can easily do that. Still, I think to myself that I just want to try a small turn by only using a little finger on the rein, and the horse bolts straight away. Under normal circumstances, I would try to stop it immediately, but it has run off because I have made only a slight movement with the reins. I sit there for a few seconds considering what I should do. It makes a U-turn – I know that because I can see a brief picture of myself floating up in the air as it turns – and then I fall to the ground. The owner and my friend who was going to buy the horse say they have seen many falls and accidents but they have never heard anything as violent as when I fell off. I don't know how I hit the ground because I faint and can't remember. Luckily, I am wearing a safety vest and a brand-new riding helmet, but I am so dizzy that I don't even notice that I have lost one of the lenses from my glasses, even though I have minus nine in strength. I try to get to my feet, but I can't. I crawl over to the fence and sit there for a long time before I am driven first back to the yard with my riding gear and then home to my husband, who drives me to the hospital. Here I am examined and given a note that says something in Latin and then a brochure that says, 'You have hit your head; you have to take it easy.' The next day my husband drives me to the optician, and from there I have to walk 200 metres to the library, where my husband is waiting in the meantime. I am surprised to find that I can't walk there. But I have been pulling myself together all my life, and I do that now too.

In bed for months

I do far too much the first week after the accident because I don't know that I have concussion – that was what was written in Latin on my injury report, but no one had said it out loud to me. Even though I was supposed to relax, I take a few days off in the summer cottage with my in-laws, who have a dog to look after and a nephew who is noisy. I don't look after myself in any way, shape or form, as I am also the one who grills the food. Sweet Sarah takes care of everything as usual.

After a week like that, I am unable to do anything. I can't walk, I can't sit up long enough to eat my fill, and I can't look out the window for as much as a brief moment. When I cross my boundaries, I can only lie down and throw up in the bathroom all night. Yet I am still the optimist, and I am the one who has to keep the mood up for my husband and my 17-year-old daughter, who are worried.

In the end, I get driven to hospital again and only here do I find out I have concussion. I am sent straight home to bed and I lie here for several months. I borrow a couple of crutches so that I can get into the living room and my husband both makes breakfast and sandwiches for me before he goes to work. One day he forgets, and I have to eat some dry crispbread for lunch because I'm so cognitively impaired that I can't use a knife. I can't put two identical socks together or put my food in the microwave either. I can only lie down or sit. My big dream becomes that I can just walk around my house once. I also still dream of getting back to my job as a lawyer and working full time, even though I don't even have a life at home. My employers are very generous and wait a long time before I get the nicest dismissal and then an early retirement. I howl when the pension comes – that isn't what I wanted.

Two deaths and a lecture

In the following years, my husband takes care of everything. The only thing I can do is ride. But in 2015, he dies suddenly and a month later my first horse has to be put down. The vet is very solicitous and takes care of both the horse and its owner, and she asks me if I have considered clairvoyant advice. I have, but it seems like a jungle to me. The vet tells me about the lectures Marzcia gives, and I get some friends to drive me there. One evening, Marzcia tells me that she isn't taking any more people for healing, but she says that everyone can learn to heal. During the break that day, my friend and I sign up for the next Reiki 1. I can sense that it has to be her, even though she lives far away from me. All in all, I have always had a good intuition and have also used it, at work for example, but without being aware that I am using my intuition.

In November 2016, I start on Reiki 1. At the training, there is a day of teaching followed by 21 practice days where I have to heal myself until I go back to teaching. In the periods when I am healing myself, I can really feel that tensions are disappearing and that it is really good for me. It goes from me being able to do nothing to today where I can do, not everything, but a great deal. Healing takes place layer by layer. If you have pain in your knees, there may be four traumas you need to have resolved before you get to the pain that you came for in the first place. But it is constantly moving forward. When we are going to the second day of the course, I try to drive a small part of the way myself but have to give up and hand over the steering wheel to my friend. But already the next time I go to a course with Marzcia, I manage to drive all the way. Admittedly, I have food and clothing with me in case I have to rest for a few hours, but I don't need them. It is great even though I am tired and have to overnight halfway.

Ten years younger

I take one course after another and, during that period, when I meet people who haven't seen me for a while, they often say: 'My God, I couldn't see it was you – you look ten years younger.' At the same time as I progress physically, I also get to know myself. On the Reiki training, Marzcia says that all of us in the circle are sensitive and I think that for me, that is only because of the accident. But it gradually dawns on me that I have always been not just sensitive, but super-sensitive. I just haven't been listening to myself, nor have I been taking care of myself but of everyone else. I also take the clairvoyance training and, during a clairvoyance with a client, I get a picture of an oxygen mask dropping in a plane. I could use that myself! I have always given the oxygen mask to others before myself. Gradually, I learn how sensitive and vulnerable I really am and that being like that is okay. Where I grew up, crying was forbidden. I therefore hid my tears as a child because if I showed them, I would be labelled as weak. But now I am beginning to realise that being vulnerable is not a weakness but a strength because I am helping both myself and others through that vulnerability.

Crying over Gabriel

The spiritual path helps me because it introduces me to an alternative place. It is like having a fairy-tale world. The first time I am on an angel course and sense the archangel Gabriel, I am in floods of tears. I simply feel him rocking me in his arms; it might as well have been physical. You can't get that kind of care and love from a psychologist. You can get an insight and that is important too. I went to a really good psychologist when my husband died. But this is learning by doing – you experience it all over your body. Before, I was very much in my head. Now I have to listen to my body and the spirit world gives me a way to do it. It gives me the tools to fill myself with light, love and energy so that I actually have something to give.

I get closer to myself and my soul essence, a process that is continuing. Even when I die it won't end because then I will just continue working in my next life!

A good life without hamster wheels
I think I have a good life today. I have a horse, I meditate a lot, and I spend a lot of time with crystals. When I hold one, it is like holding a beating heart. I also do a little bit of healing and clairvoyance. I see slightly fewer people than before where I was a party animal and was always inviting people to dinner. Some of my old friends think I'm a little crazy because I have this interest; others are more open, and I am still making new spiritual friends. And then I have two grandchildren, the oldest of whom is six. When he was a baby, my husband had to drive me over to be with him once a week, and when my husband died, I had to come and visit my grandson myself for a short time each visit. Later I would pick him up and be with him on the playground. But today I can simply fetch him, drive him home to my place, eat with him and drive him home again. I had never thought that would happen. I also thought it was over with travelling, even though I loved it, but I've been on two charter holidays with my daughter. Something like that means a great deal to me. There are many times where I have thought of the accident

that happened thirteen years ago with gratitude. Of course, I would rather not have been through it because it has been so hard, but today I wouldn't have my old job back. I have found that I can't mentally and physically live in a hamster wheel. I need peace and to sit by myself in perfect peace. I can no longer throw myself into things as I have been doing all my life.

Not without spirituality

That I have come this far is clearly due to the healing. I may well have a fighting spirit, but it could never have taken me this far on its own. With my fighting spirit, I would have been able to walk again, to look out the window a little and maybe just be with my grandchild for a short time. Healing has taught me what I can and can't bear – and has taught me to look after myself. I had no idea I had boundaries, which meant that people crossed them all the time. If I hadn't found a way into myself and found respect for myself and my boundaries, I would have continued to be run over. That realisation, knowledge and way of feeling wouldn't come to me with fighting spirit. That today I can feel surrounded by love and use it to be refilled – that doesn't come from fighting spirit. The fact that I go into some karmic or epigenetic life – or just an ordinary healing – means that I let go of some of the burdens I carry around with me. I have been extremely prone to taking on too much responsibility; a good example is that some people have seen me in visions carrying the whole planet on my shoulders, and that is heavy! Before, I would get ill when I went over my own boundaries. Today I can better distinguish between what is good for me and what isn't. Or who is good for whom. My relationships have changed so that I am more able to say no to friends or family. There are also people I meet where I think, 'I'm not having anything more to do with you.' In the past, they just might have come close into my life and drained me. Before, I said to my friends, 'Do you want something? Well, you can have it. I give you everything.' If I had continued without all these insights and experiences, I think I would have kept fleeing from myself. At one point, I was drinking a little too much, but today I can get a buzz out of meditating. Here I am not fleeing, but, on the contrary, I go into myself and feel myself. I don't know how long I would have lived if I hadn't got into this."

***

CHAPTER 4 – in brief

- As human beings, we all have some tensions, blockages or even traumas that stand in the way of us being able to live in harmony with our innermost core, our soul essence. A trauma occurs at boundaries that are suddenly broken, either in our thoughts, feelings or bodies, so that we shut down parts of ourselves. It makes sense to shut down right when the break happens, but later it may be inappropriate with those locked areas. We become limited in our lives and there is not enough space to live as we are.
- The human autonomic nervous system can be divided into the sympathetic, which is the fight-or-flight mode, and the parasympathetic, which is calmness, digestion and rest. The ability to switch between the sympathetic system and the parasympathetic system is the ability to bring oneself to a calm state, for example after a violent physical and/or emotional experience.
- Peter A. Levine is a pioneer in shock/trauma theory and is the man behind the Somatic Experiencing® method (SE). The principle behind SE is that one works with the trauma

through the body, the feelings and the beliefs by gently approaching the trauma and gradually dissolving it. The theories are based partly on studies of wild animals, which literally shake off violent experiences by shaking accumulated energy and locked positions out of their bodies and nervous systems.

- We humans have natural instincts like animals and, like them, react by fleeing, fighting or freezing when there is danger. But unlike the animals, because of the neocortex in the cerebral cortex of our brain, we can repress our natural instincts. We can remain static when we really want to flee, or we can go into freeze-mode when we ought to be fighting. When we are "forced" to it, however, our instincts continue to run within us – we "flee from the lion," even though there isn't one. We become traumatised.

- Ever since we were babies, our nervous systems have been orientating themselves towards the loving presence of our caregivers. We are used to connecting with and regulating ourselves according to other people's nervous systems, and that ability means that the healing presence is able to support the client when the client's nervous system connects with the help and presence of the spirit world.

- As a healer, I combine my knowledge from Peter A. Levine's methods, Susan Hart's work on mirror neurons and Bruce Lipton's cell biology theory with help from healing and the spirit world. The healing presence collaborates with the client's self-healing potential and puts the client in a calm state from which the trauma or blockages can be processed. In this way, there is extra support in the form of angels, guides, deceased relatives and above all a divine presence, which is also within the client herself, in the soul essence.

**AT MARZCIA.DK YOU CAN
FIND THESE MEDITATIONS:**

Liberation from being stuck

Contact your spiritual guides

CHAPTER 5

YOUR INNER CHILD

*About working with the trauma when and
where it occurred*

When I was five, my parents bought an orchard. They dreamt of cultivating the land, keeping animals and living from it – that was in the 1970s – but for various reasons, they ended up having to give up the orchard. Later, they got a farm where they realised all their plans. But their first disappointment, pain, and giving up on the orchard took up residence within me. I felt the energy in the family and embedded a sense that things wouldn't work out no matter what I did. The experience wasn't really mine, it was my parents', but it sat in me anyway. I was little and didn't know that everything would be fine again. I gained the belief that if I relaxed just for a moment, everything would fall apart. I came to struggle with enormous exhaustion later in life, which had to do with this period and which actually didn't fit with the adult Marzcia at all. During a year of intense healing much later in adulthood, I resolved both the belief and the exhaustion, and I learned to distinguish when I came up against the feeling of performance demands or exhaustion: Is this the five-year-old Marzcia or the one who is ten times as old? This, in its essence, is what inner child-work is all about.

***

In order for you to thrive, feel safe, maintain good contact with yourself and others, feel present and stay grounded in your life, it is crucial that in your early development you have had the opportunity to develop your skills and grow up and further develop them. If you haven't had this, healing of inner child states could help you a lot. It is never too late to have a good childhood. Happy, safe and vibrant inner children grow up well and give corresponding strength, vitality, joy of life and access to your essence in the adult-you today.

***

Inner child healing can make a crucial difference if you have any of the following conditions:

- A highly sensitive nervous system, which quickly comes into an alarm state (sympathetic nervous system response), and you have difficulty returning to a calm and safe state of rest/recharging (parasympathetic nervous system).
- You have challenges with attachment and setting boundaries in relationships, both in close, private relationships and, for example, work relationships.
- You have challenges with feeling part of the physical, lived life, a sense of not being welcome and entitled to be here. Even if you want to be a part of the community, you can't break through your inner wall and people have a hard time getting close to you. In short, social relationships are a challenge.
- You are easily influenced by the attitudes, moods and emotions of others.
- You have a basic feeling of not belonging, of not being rooted in yourself, life and the world.
- You are in doubt about who you are or you have a negative and deficient self-image.
- You have a deep longing for home, but since you don't find home in yourself in the physical life, you seek home in others, in physical places, in your thoughts, in your work or in the spirit world.

This chapter comes with suggestions about some of the causes of these conditions and, not least, how you can begin to heal the process of "growing up."

A NERVOUS SYSTEM IN ALARM

In SE, which I told you about in Chapter 4, we work with the concept of Global High Intensity Activation (GHIA), a state with a very high level of activation of your nervous system. In this state, you find it easy to be on the alert, but difficult to settle. Either you are at full speed with a lot of alarm, or you are completely exhausted. This occurs if there is intense stress, either physical or emotional, in the foetal stage, during birth or in the new-born baby. The little child can't get away from being influenced nor can it fight against influences. Nor can she nurse or comfort herself because, as children, we are completely dependent on another nervous system or a calm comforting presence to be able to settle. This means that the little child goes into a frozen state or shuts down and gives up, while any excess energy is distributed to the organs, intestines, spine and nervous system. This condition can cause many problems of a physical, mental and emotional nature throughout life. Though the connection between the soul and the body is complicated, security and peace can be achieved by addressing a tense, alarmed nervous system that causes the person to be in survival mode or completely closed off inside. This, in turn, is an explanation for the fact that what you have experienced very early in your life continues to affect you and possibly keeps you in a state of alarm, which is very exhausting for the whole you.

If you start working on healing your inner child, you will find that your nervous system begins to relax. The old nerve pathways of alarm response will be toned down and new nerve pathways will grow. Your posture and muscle mass will change, and often your immune system will also change positively. It is wearing on the body, in fact on the whole system, to be in a state of alarm all the time, so changing your state to one of more peace, joy and security – a security in yourself – will mean that your resources will be used to rebuild you instead of on maintaining a tiring alarm state. New neurons, nerve pathways, muscles and beliefs begin to grow. You will be in your life as an adult with more contact to yourself.

FOUR IMPORTANT PERIODS

Inner-child work is a form of healing that heals the younger you. It matters a great deal whether a lockdown or a shutdown happened when you were lying in your mother's womb, when you had just started school, when you were in puberty or in your late teens. Each age has its typical issues, which come along in step with our mental, emotional and physical development. In my inner-child healing course, I generally divide childhood into four periods, namely:

- From the foetal state up to about 1 year old
- From about 1 year old to about 5 years old
- School age up to early teens (6–12 years old)
- The teenage years

Each period has its own challenges in terms of integrating you and your soul essence into your life and your body. Thus, when we go back and look at when certain, locked positions or beliefs have come into our lives, we can work very precisely with the healing of that trauma or that belief.[5]

WHEN THE SOUL MEETS THE CHILD

Your physical life begins with the fertilisation of an egg by a sperm. Once the fertilised egg has embedded itself in the uterus, it lies there growing for nine months – like the yolk of an egg. We all know that, but I would still like to dwell a little on how you wrote yourself into an incredibly long story when you came into being – again.

INNER CHILD - TRAUMA
0-6 YEARS OLD

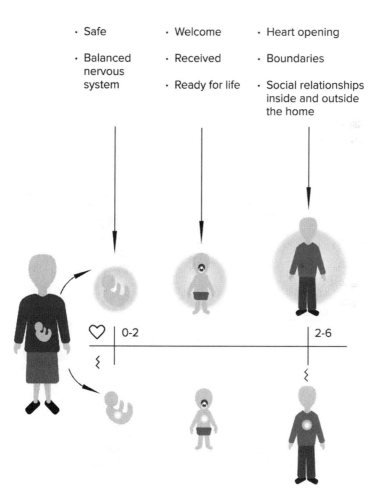

- Safe
- Balanced nervous system

- Welcome
- Received
- Ready for life

- Heart opening
- Boundaries
- Social relationships inside and outside the home

In the case of trauma, survival strategies will take over and the integration of the soul essence will be reduced.

INNER CHILD - TRAUMA
6-19 YEARS OLD

· Good balance in
  heart and brain

· Social learning
  inside and outside
  the home

· Heart opening

· Identity

· Independence

· Boundaries

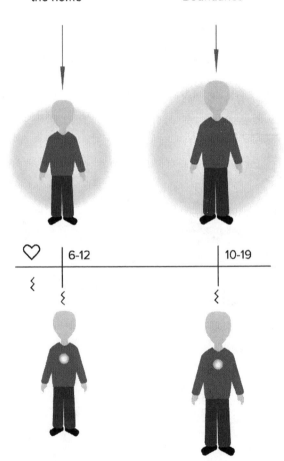

In the case of trauma, survival strategies will take over
and the integration of the soul essence will be reduced.

We can say that, as foetuses, we go through the entire history of human development, from tadpoles to multicellular creatures, in the nine months we lie growing in the womb. It happens every single day, but it is in fact a miracle that carries with it the whole history of the Earth and humanity. We were once single-celled organisms; we have been reptiles and mammals and have gradually become human beings. It all lies in our genes. Our lineage has survived because the collaboration between our souls and our bodies has been well developed over millions of years. It works, and our task is to get the best out of it. But if the collaboration is blocked from the foetal state, it becomes difficult. During this period, your soul needs to descend again from the soul home and collaborate with a body, and it can be quite challenging to get from the light, fine vibration of consciousness to the heavier physical vibration of life on Earth.

Fortunately, we are never alone in this difficult process. There is a whole network around us to help: both our closest physical relatives and several different levels from the spirit world. For example, you always have a team of guides and angels and a guardian guide who will support you, not only at the beginning of your life, but always. It is often easier for you to be in touch with some spiritual levels than others. For some it is Jesus, God, the Virgin Mary, angels; for others it is guides; for still others it may be elves or other beings in nature; and for others again, it is dead people and ancestors who provide the necessary loving support. Whomever it is, in the spirit world, towards which we prefer to orientate ourselves is very much about that which our soul essence is composed. Just as our DNA is our genetic imprint, our inheritance from our lineage, the "DNA" of our soul, is composed of divine essence and various "strings" from the various spiritual levels, as well as from the experiences we have had in past lives. Depending on the particular composition of your soul, you will automatically have a closer contact with some parts of the spirit world, and they will be able to support you the most.[6]

Although there are many interconnections of souls and bodies every day and we have massive help, it can be a difficult process when the new child and its soul have to merge. It may be due to difficulties in the actual coupling between soul and incarnate human being. As a soul, you have an ability to be in contact with something very deep, loving, essential and divine, because your soul contains all those elements. The soul then has to collaborate with the physical body and its reactions to the themes, epigenetic and karmic and to the environment. The nervous system, feelings and beliefs can have difficulty accommodating or opening up to the finer parts of the soul consciousness. Maybe you even land in something that is a bit chaotic. Thus, there may already be beliefs in the style of "Phew, now I can remember what it was like – I'm off," which means that parts of the soul have not incarnated. The soul is always full of desire to experience and contribute, but reality isn't always so rosy. Past experiences of being overwhelmed or past traumas and your mother's traumas are like vibrations on their way down towards physical moorings. Perhaps the soul has looked forward to coming down and working on a theme of powerlessness because it didn't finish it the last time, but when it comes down, parts of the old, unprocessed consciousness of what it really was like to experience powerlessness are activated in the body, which can then shut parts of the soul out.

COMPLETELY DEPENDENT ON MUM

The problem can also arise in the particular circumstances which you come down into. The soul comes from a deep security and safety in the closeness it has had with other souls in the soul home. Now it has to go down and work with Mum's eggs and Dad's sperm, and suddenly you become dependent on the nourishment you get from your Mum. Your body is going to begin shaping itself from your mother's energy, and that in which you land is therefore everything that your mother has with her of moods and feelings, unprocessed or even traumatic stuff. Because you are so dependent on your mother, you easily take over her beliefs, feelings and energies. Your cells are made up of a mixture of your mother's and father's genes, but the nourishment from your mother and the environment of the womb in which you were lying is most important for your growth and your development at this stage of your life. In this state, you can incorporate your mother's themes a little too much and it can both cause a complicated mother relationship and a lot of trouble for you to address later. It is one thing to work with your own themes, but it is another to work with your mother's without even knowing they belong to her.

Other influences may also come into play. Maybe there are tensions between your Mum and Dad. Maybe they are going through something intense or difficult while your mother is pregnant. Or something is happening around them. All of this affects you and can make it more difficult for you to integrate your soul essence from the start.

OVER-RESPONSIBLE, SENSITIVE OR INSECURE?

Everything that happens in the first period of your physical existence belongs to the time before your mental memory and language. You can't remember it with your thoughts or words, because you don't have them yet, but the blockages may lie in your cells, muscles and nervous system as beliefs or themes. Certain themes often stem from the early days, over-responsibility, the feeling of not being strong enough to be in the world or insecurity. Let's say you have a tendency to be over-responsible; it makes sense, because when you were a foetus, you were completely dependent on the survival of others for your own survival, so you literally had to take care of others first, and you might still be doing that. It may also be that you have a feeling that you mustn't be in the world unless you take care of other people, just as you had to back then. Or you have a very intense nervous system that can play games with you because you tend to feel overwhelmed or be overstimulated – or conversely, you have completely shut down your senses because you can't cope with it all. It all fits very well with having physical form. Insecurity can also be part of this theme. Even though you were surrounded by amniotic fluid in the womb, you may have felt completely unprotected. Perhaps because you have come from something very beautiful in the soul home to something less loving and much more chaotic in your new life.

If you have themes like these and they originate from the foetal state, they are impossible to find linguistically because you didn't have language at the time. You only had your nervous system, which orientated itself to your surroundings, that is, your mother. You were in a pure state of being, and if being there was not particularly nice, you only had the possibility of refraining from incarnating with much of your soul essence, which would be able to feel that discomfort. One possibility was to leave part of the soul essence out. When you let a little of your soul essence disappear, you have a hard time sensing your own essence and the influence of others comes to fill you. At the same time, you get a preponderance of survival mechanisms, oftentimes causing a really difficult, challenging life – unless, of course, you re-establish yourself and gain access to the flame of your soul consciousness within, which can radiate out and heal you from within and without.

People with high sensitivity often find that it has been too overwhelming to step into the general stew of life on Earth. But once they get over that hurdle, they have an intense amount to radiate out into the world that can help others who are having a difficult time being in this life. They can help humanity lift itself up. If that is how you feel, there is good reason to work with your inner child, both for your own sake and for the sake of others. You have a lot to contribute.

THE FOETAL STATE

In the foetal state, it is a lot about not being able to find peace and the feeling of being allowed to be in the world, so if these are some of your themes, it will be really good to work with this state. Imagine that the foetus needs to be detoxified from that which creates discomfort in the body, the feelings or the mind. It can be old stress from your mother: that is, something epigenetic or karmic. The crucial thing is that the foetus becomes secure by incorporating the soul essence in peace, love and security. When you, as a child, are placed in a state of security, it is like recreating a safe foetal state and keeping out what has been causing stress. The foetus can thereby grow and there is better contact with your soul essence and you can grow from there. You get a feeling of being able to be safe, open and receptive, without it meaning that something bad comes in – and improve at sensing and opening yourself to a loving presence. Conversely, if it wasn't good for you back then, today you may not have trust in something good coming to you. This stage then becomes very much about being safe and having the trust that you are welcome here and that the nervous system can calm down so that you can land in bodily contact with yourself. This is really important in order to learn how to regulate your nervous system. Already at this point, the collaboration with your guardian angel can be good because you as a foetus become safe and well, and the early alarm systems are being regulated. You get new nerve pathways and you can better digest the day. In short, you feel "as snug as a bug in a rug." You are taken care of and have a basic trust in growing up in the world.

HEALING OF THE INNER CHILD
BLOCKAGE FROM FOETAL STATE

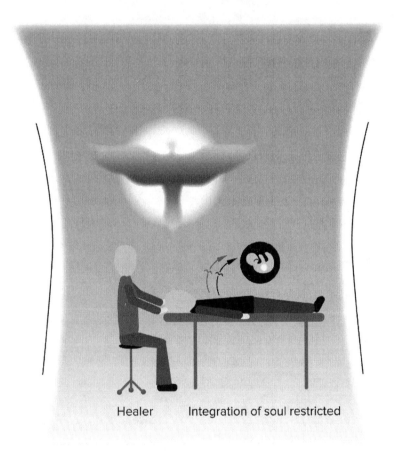

Healer   Integration of soul restricted

HEALING OF THE INNER CHILD
MORE OF THE SOUL IS INTEGRATED

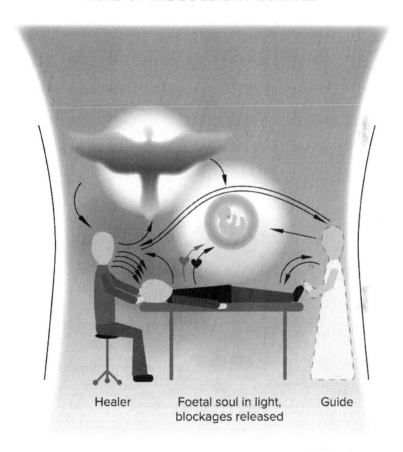

Healer   Foetal soul in light,   Guide
          blockages released

HEALING OF THE INNER CHILD

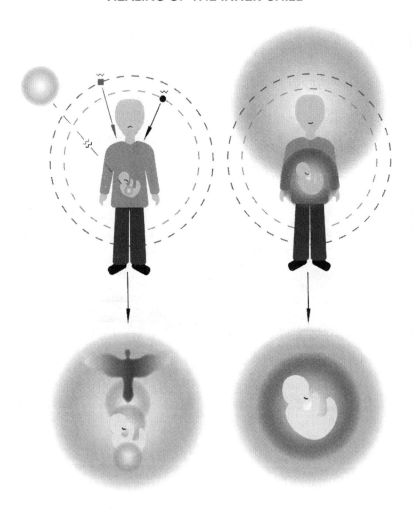

THE BIRTH STATE

When you are ready to be born, you have turned round inside your mother and are being pushed out by the contractions and by using your legs which you are pressing against your mother's diaphragm. It is your first real use of your power in life – it is a matter of life or death. In the old days especially, both mothers and children died during childbirth, and even though we have many ways to avoid that in our part of the world today, childbirth is still a physical and psychological test of whether you are strong enough to use your body and get out. If it goes well, you will come out with a physical strength and a feeling of being able to master what it takes to be a physical being. A big wail comes out of you as you get rid of the frustrations of being born; it wasn't nice, but you succeeded. You cease to be enveloped in fluid and come out into pure air where you have no sense of your physical shape. At this point, it is important that you are touched so that you gain the ability to cope with the transition. A sense of security and trust in oneself arises; you relax and the soul essence can come in again. If, on the other hand, it doesn't go all that smoothly, there will be times during your birth where you get a shock or trauma – for example, the feeling of being pressed or decidedly lacking oxygen. If those experiences don't fall properly into place, you will continue to have those traumas. During birth you have dissociated with some of your soul essence, some parts have, so to speak, disappeared during birth so you can't get them back. If you are to be healed of this, there must be an extreme slowness and strong support, for example, with the help of a healer, an SE therapist or similar. Here the body may do some of the things you did during a birth – push with your legs, get exhausted and so on.

When you come out, it is important that you feel welcome and held. If there has been disturbance around this part of the birth and, for example, you have been taken over to an examination immediately, the secure state when coming out doesn't occur. Then you have to go back and heal it because it is about being welcome in the world. If there is trauma, the coupling with your soul essence may have a hard time working at that point. The fusion between body and more of the soul can be difficult. Your nervous system and your body haven't calmed down completely and become deeply relaxed, and the soul can't be fully integrated. That point is really important for the feeling of surrendering yourself to care; you can also go back and heal that.

YOU ARE THE LITTLE CHILD AND THE LITTLE CHILD IS YOU

In inner child work, it is important to remember that the little child is you and you are the little child. Everything you have had with you through life comes in direct contact with what existed before you were born, with pregnancy and childbirth and all the way up to where you are today. When you connect with your soul's journey through life, you are strengthened in your connection with yourself. The little child, who, either in the foetal state or at birth, has felt that everything was going wrong, can now notice that it in fact worked because you're here, you have grown up. There is a reciprocity and love in meeting yourself, which is part of the healing work in which the spirit world envelops and supports the fusion of the little child's soul-essence and the adult soul-essence so that they become one flame. This means that your soul essence is allowed to radiate even more because the old blockages fall away.

Birth is therefore important to work with in order to have confidence in getting through, being prepared and feeling welcome. Being a new-born has to do with being in strong survival mode, and it can be hard to be able to accept, to say yes to life and feel comfortable in one's body if something has gone wrong at this point. It also provides access to the soul awareness plane. The soul has been there all along, but it can be difficult to establish contact with it. The first months before we are born and after we are born are, in short, about mastering the task of being alive.

LOVE IN THE LINEAGE IS A PROTECTION AGAINST FOETAL STRESS

At a lecture on inner child states, a pregnant woman came up to me and was afraid that she had harmed her child because she and her boyfriend had gone their separate ways during pregnancy. I asked her if she could feel her foetus, and she lit up in the most beautiful, loving smile. So even though she was sad and had her own challenges, she had enveloped her child with so much love that it could come into the world safely. As I stood talking to her, her late grandmother came forward and stood behind her, so that she enveloped both her granddaughter and her great-granddaughter with the same loving, gentle state of presence. I asked the woman if she could sense her grandmother, and she could – there were tears and emotion. The great-grandmother helped both the great-grandchild to be attached to its mother and her grandchild to be attached to her child. The story is a good example of how, when there is lots of love present, the child can handle a certain amount of pressure. The great-grandmother would now go with her grandchild and great-grandchild and be with them for the rest of the pregnancy, and I am sure it is still going really well for them. For me, it was also a really good example that we are never alone, neither as foetuses nor as adults. Help is there when we need it.

THE EARLY YEARS: THE HEART IS OPENED

In the first years of our lives, we are deeply dependent on our parents. Now we are in the world, but we can't do anything ourselves; we can't get food for ourselves and we can't regulate our own nervous systems. The skin is our contact with the world, and we literally live from feeling someone touching us. We need to be held, spoken to gently, sung to and comforted to calm down. When a baby cries, or a small child stretches up with its arms, there has to be someone who picks it up, otherwise the child can't survive.

Themes that originate from the very early years include the feeling of not knowing where you yourself begin and end, that is, the important boundaries that are now defined by touches on the skin. You feel like there are no boundaries, you can't find your own boundaries or you are going to cross over other peoples'. Abandonment is also a prevalent feeling that can occur here; you lift your arms but no one is there to pick you up. At this point in your life, you have been away from the spirit world for a relatively long time. If the spirit world isn't so present to you because you have to integrate on the physical plane and at the same time there isn't the necessary support here, than your nervous system gets help to feel safe, and the soul can't get in properly.

MY EARLY INNER-CHILD WORK

In my own life, I have been through several intense things very early on. I was born with the umbilical cord around my neck and my mother had to be moved in the middle of giving birth. My dad can't remember anything of it, even though he was present, and I think he was in a state of shock at that moment. He usually has a really good memory. When I was one and a half years old, my mother became very ill with a kidney disease. She underwent surgery and was away convalescing for several weeks. Naturally, this meant that I became more attached to my father during that period, and when my mother returned, it was difficult to open up and receive the love she had for me. Much later in my life, I came in contact with a belief from that time that my mother was dead and out of my life. The little one-year-old in me had simply gone through the grieving process and had closed off part of my heart.

The need for closeness was difficult for the little girl I was back then – she was simply afraid to open up and receive again. This period in my early life has created a lot of pain between my mother and me, both because my mother felt that the little girl from that time rejected her and because the little girl I once was has felt a lack of care and a big loss. The two blockages were getting in the way. Behind it, of course, there has always been love and the desire for connectedness – like two magnets that seek each other and yet repel each other, without either of us wanting to deep down. It is a great joy for me and probably also my mother, when the deeper meeting, the deeper-lying love from soul to soul, succeeds in flowing through the blockages and creating the good experiences, the healing connectedness and the experiences we have fortunately also had to build on.

Immediately after my mother became ill, one of the dogs to which I was very attached was put down, and shortly thereafter I developed German measles and severe pneumonia and had to be hospitalised for a long time. For several reasons, my parents couldn't be there. My grandparents were there, but at that time relatives were only allowed to come during visiting hours. My grandmother has told me that I had changed completely after I came home from hospital. It has thus been the last straw for how much anxiety, sadness and feelings of abandonment my system could take.

Because of these episodes, among other things, I have had to work a lot with the younger versions of myself to dare to open up to love and the vulnerability I had automatically shut down to protect myself very early. It has been very conscious personal work for me throughout my life, because my vulnerability and opening myself to receive and pass on the love of the spirit world is necessary for the calling and the work I have. It has meant a lot of self-healing, various courses of therapy, spiritual development, security with animals and the spirit world and not least a lovingly supportive and patient spouse which has enabled me to do this.

There was also a lot of contact with my early foetal state and childhood when I had a hammock installed on our very small balcony. The state I got into by lying in it was the starting shot for even deeper contact with a sense of peace and presence from the cradle; my nervous system remembered the condition, and suddenly I had an extra opportunity to get in contact with my parasympathetic nervous system. The extra peace helped me get even more in touch with my inner essence and a feeling of being able to be comfortable in being at home in myself. Logically, I could tell my system that right now there was no danger going on or anything vital I had forgotten or should do. It was okay not to be in a state of alarm. Infra-red saunas, hot baths, the flames and heat from fires, soft fabrics and gentle physical and emotional presence all helped too. Many of these states recur in the healing meditations I sense from the spirit world to myself or others.

LOVE AND THE SEARCH FOR BOUNDARIES

When we reach the age of two to five, we can get around, express needs and engage in a form of dialogue. The earlier state, where it was impossible to get away physically, is over. The little child begins to reconnoitre, explore the world and test boundaries. It tries to get beyond them, feel what it is like out there (which might trigger a howl of fright or frustration at being interrupted by Mum or Dad) and get back to safety again. This age is really important for self-perception and social relationships later in life. This is what some call the age of defiance, which is about exploring and examining, seeking boundaries and creating boundaries, sensing oneself and others. At the same time, there are huge heart-opening opportunities here. The two to three-year-old is struggling to become herself and doesn't know that there is a long way to go before she is independent of her parents. At the same time, the emotional capacity (the neurons) is growing enormously during this period. No one can look at you like a toddler can, with infinite love in their eyes and say, "I LOVE you, Mum/Dad/Auntie/big brother," and in kindergarten "sweetheart relationships" and friendships arise that are really deeply felt and for life – at least, as far as these little hearts can see it at this point. The small children really love their adults and each other, and here it is possible to be in good contact with the soul essence and also both to feel loved and to love. The appetite for life and the drive there is, at this point, important, but the child is still deeply reflecting its parents and everything that happens around them. Being able to be out and experience and to come home in a safe and reassuring embrace is also very important during this period. It is also important at that age that boundaries are set in a good way so that the child both learns to set boundaries itself and that there are boundaries for it. It can therefore also have significance far into adulthood if something happens in the child's relationships at this point that isn't being processed. Since the heart is so open, the child can be really hurt, and it can later mean that your love energy cannot flow out into the world. It can be difficult to accommodate big, loving feelings if they haven't been taken care of when you were little. Remember that soul is feelings and consciousness. As a three-year-old, you really train the big emotions – to be extremely angry, excessively happy or deeply in love. It is really good to feel these feelings so you can later accommodate and express those feelings in a balanced way. In ordinary upbringing, we often talk about setting boundaries, but if a child can express its feelings and feel its own boundaries, it doesn't become boundary-breaking; it is about balance. This calmness with the big emotions, the security of the setting and the loving togetherness and connectedness with the surroundings give space for your nervous system to relax. The little child trains her contact with her soul essence and her survival responses from the body's survival strategies. If you didn't get a good balance in your system when you were little, some negative survival patterns will take up a large part of the space, and other good states will have much less space – not enough, in fact, for you to escape the survival pressure and achieve more peace, openness of heart and contact with your soul essence. You are going to live from your place of survival rather than from your true essence. We need both of them to survive and live, so the balance and being able to switch from one state to another is crucial.

WHEN GRANDMA OR THE DOG DIES

Since the heart opening is so intense during this period, losses that don't get attention may come to affect you later. If a friend moves, or a pet or a grandparent dies, the adults aren't always aware of how important it is to work with the child's pain. The conversation about grief may have been there, but the process is rushed through: "That was a few days ago; let's not talk about it any more." To an adult, a dead rabbit or a friend having moved away may seem like a trifle, but it is far from a trifle for a child because we are created to be connected. When we are separated from, for example, a little friend, a small part of our heart is actually torn out. This doesn't mean that losses in themselves are dangerous; experiencing being separated from those we love is a part of life, and that doesn't mean that love disappears. The soul contact will always be there, even if we are physically separated. As we mature, we learn to take this calmly – that is, if we are lovingly helped through the first losses. If we aren't, we can later become afraid of losing people, so we either don't attach ourselves to anyone or attach ourselves to other people in a way that is too intense. We can become so afraid of losing someone that our world collapses at the slightest rejection. In this case, a later healing through contact with the dead can help a great deal because it supports us in feeling that connectedness doesn't stop because a human being isn't physically present. The opening that Grandma or your little rabbit made in your heart made you able to love. You can use the positive opening that has happened to heal the closure. In general, big losses of various kinds throughout your childhood will make a strong impact.

OUT INTO THE WORLD

At this age and beyond, you also go further out into the world beyond your own little nuclear family. Perhaps you start in a nursery or kindergarten and have to gain experience on your own and create relationships outside the home. It holds great potential; little friends or a loving nursery worker or day-care provider can show you that love also exists outside of the family and that is a wonderful experience to have. The can-do-spirit and self-confidence of a three-year-old is wonderful, but you may also experience disappointments and rejections that can set in and stifle your can-do-spirit. You may begin doubting that other people really want to be with you and you may become resigned in relation to your own need to be met and seen. Intense emotional experiences can become strongly imprinted in your beliefs and mean that you will shut off from receiving love. This makes things difficult for the open, emotionally secure part of you, that is, the wonderful can-do-spirit, self-confidence and the more positive matter-of-factness that life is good, the world is safe, and other people can receive what you have to offer.

This can mean that, over time, you develop different patterns to gain recognition, or you find new ways to replace love or feel filled up. The need for security and love can be transferred to other areas of your life such as diet, work, sex, problems with relating to others and much more.

The big themes in the early years are love and moving a little out into the world, and it becomes even more pronounced when you approach school age and really have to go out on your own while still being dependent on your family. Here it becomes clear whether you are thriving well at home and/or outside – now and later in your life. If you have good relationships at school, you will often also thrive in your work later. Your work becomes a reflection of your time at school. And if you have problems thriving in close relationships, it will often point back at your family. You can use this as a benchmark to find out when something in particular "went wrong."

AT SCHOOL: FAREWELL TO SENSITIVITY AND SPIRITUALITY

When you start school, you step into a society that doesn't have much room for spirituality, for being in your soul essence and for having as many feelings as you may have been used to having in your early childhood. Now sitting and fondling a stone for hours or talking about the angels you see is no longer approved. Since there is so much you have to learn – to sit still and listen to the teacher; to read, write and count – you get exposed to an over-programming in being in your brain and thoughts and having to understand and keep up. In fact, you now have to fit into a very square shape, just a few years after you were in the soul home as a completely free being. In that way, it can be said that you will be adapted to something other than what is normal and healthy for you. In school, there is not much room for the tools that help you calm down and regenerate – being a creative, soft, loving and gentle presence who is in spiritual contact with your soul or unfolding yourself physically – because the academic subjects take up so much space in the education system today. Everything that is important for you to get in place as a child – to draw and paint or to run and use your body, to have time that is not scheduled, but where contemplation, spontaneity and intuition can fit in – is screened out. You quite simply lose some points of reference. There is no room to quietly meditate by yourself, in contact with your soul.

Herein lies a risk of losing yourself and the breadth of your capacity because you get away from the body and the feelings and up into the head. Your ability to recharge is reduced, just as the healthy dialogue with the soul consciousness and the spirit world is reduced. This means you may lose touch with your inner core.

Good relationships with your teacher and classmates will mean that the security, joy and trust in relationships will continue. Unfortunately, there is often a lot of trauma associated with bullying, exclusion or bad experiences with teachers, which in turn can negatively affect your trust in relationships outside the home and increase feelings of inferiority. As mentioned before, your time at school often creates fertile ground for your relationship with work, career and life outside the home; it is therefore a very important period to look at if you are struggling with themes from your past. Other themes stemming from this period can be problems with being in groups or problems with being at work, for example, in the form of stress or inability to say no to colleagues and tasks. Self-esteem problems, learning problems and performance problems often lie here as well.

ADOLESCENCE: YOUR WHOLE WORLD IS QUAKING – ARE YOU IN A STRONG POSITION?

If the time between six and twelve years old brings a large growth in neurons, then adolescence does so to an even greater degree. These years will thus also mean a lot for the rest of your life. In this wild, transitional period of our lives, there is an explosion of changes. Our brains grow, our emotional capacity expands, and it can be difficult to get the soul essence involved because we are so affected by everything that is happening around us. If you don't have peace in your core because your identity is changing, you are even more sensitive to the influence of friends, families and public figures that you idolise. Girls are starting to look womanly and may be treated by others as more adult than they really are, and the boys have to be more masculine and bigger than they feel deep down. There is a lot of pressure and a performance race now that the young person is really going to make her or his mark on the world.

In many ways, the teens can be reminiscent of the early years (two to five years old). Consciousness expands once more and the young person must step out into society, just as when the three-year-old had to get used to being away from family, out into the world, and the six-year-old had to start school. The great heart openings also happen again at this time and we get the big infatuations. But as the emotional capacity grows, we can also feel all that isn't very nice to feel. And again, the young person may take in a loss very deeply, and no one will notice how upset the 13-year-old is about losing her grandfather or her dog. The same, basic reactions take place in the teenager as in the small child at the same time as new ideas and inspiration are emerging.

The period can be difficult spiritually. At this age, whilst it is true that we have confirmation of the contrary in Denmark, people in other cultures they are closer to their spirituality, contact with their soul or the divine. The citizens of Denmark are more culturally Christian. Of course, there are some priests who don't just teach the Bible from the words but also from the felt contact with God and Jesus and in meditation and in prayer that is not only said but also felt as a spiritual, emotional connection between you, your soul and God. However, there often isn't an especially spacious spirituality in the Danish national church, so as a teenager you can't enter the church with the question "Who am I?" in relation to a spiritual or soul contact. The church's inadequacy allows other influences to become all the stronger because they offer answers, albeit superficial ones. If you don't have your basic trust in place – aren't integrated with your soul essence – you become sensitive to what the surrounding society thinks and has to offer.

As a teenager, I felt a great powerlessness over whether we could survive as human beings because of the way we utilise nature's resources and the conflicts we have with each other. I was young in the 1980s, which was marked by the nuclear arms race, massive pollution, the Chernobyl accident and international conflicts. I had a deep, inner feeling of powerlessness, even though I was happy and functioning well outwardly. It was a form of depressive state that I carried with me and hid out of the way. I sometimes experience that my clients also have that type of undetected depression from precisely their teenage years.

TYPICAL THEMES IN ADOLESCENCE

Themes that relate to adolescence can be about abuse. The young person may not be fully in control of his or her own boundaries, and nor are older people. At this time, there may be identity problems and unresolved emotionally overwhelming situations or beliefs, just as there may be a sense of inferiority, lack of self-esteem, insecurity in group dynamics and anxiety about making choices. If you have the feeling of being supported and helped along the way, you will be more stable in a period that is already very unstable. The basic feeling of being loved as you are, without having to perform, is crucial to how a young person gets through adolescence; it is a good framework to support the formation of healthy boundaries physically, mentally and emotionally.

There is often a very great curiosity about spirituality and the spirit world during this period, so if you get to learn to be with your soul and the spirit world now, you will get something very important for the rest of your life. It is an opportunity to have a counterbalance to the mental emphasis and the performance race. If you don't have access to your soul consciousness, the mental part of you will begin to take over your perception of who you are, your feelings will have a hard time giving a loving counterbalance to everything that is happening and won't be able to digest all the impressions and influences that come from both inside and outside. Here contact with the peace in your soul, your intuition and the support of the spirit world is important in order to maintain your contact with the whole you. Most often I hold a Reiki-1 course for young people between 13 and 18 years old, and once for 10 to 13-year-olds, where they learn self-healing and contact with their soul. They learn how to connect with the pillar of light and the healing in order to find peace and get back in balance. Of course, the young people who come are often highly sensitive and have had experiences with the spirit world already. This course creates a good opportunity for them to have that contact and knowledge with them for the rest of their lives. I know that several of the young people have used this a lot and also that their peers have been very interested and curious about this. Thus, it isn't only these individuals but also their friends who get new positive knowledge instead of all the scary, unrealistic stuff they can see in series and the like in their everyday life.

HOW TO HEAL THE INNER CHILD

If you have been blocked in your development from the start, you will always have a hard time standing on your own two feet. Whether we are talking about the foetal state or adolescence, childhood is the "beginning" of life; this is where you get your "feet." The picture may be a little intense, but the good news is that we can work with what has happened, no matter when it has happened. It used to be said that it was impossible to work with very early traumas, but I see every day in my practice that this isn't true. This is because in spiritual work we don't go in through the thoughts but through the body and the feelings. We do this with the help of the spirit world, but also with the help of a nervous system that is used to orientating itself to other nervous systems. Popularly speaking, we don't sit and talk about what once happened. Instead, your system comes into contact with the event and heals it with the help of the spirit world. In this way, it is a combination of the work that Peter A. Levine did with traumatised patients and healing with support from the spirit world.

When we work with the inner child through healing, an evocative state is established where you are surrounded by the purity and tenderness you need to grow and become more robust and open. To be able to do that, we need to find out when a trauma or a fixed belief arose. For example, if you have a particular pattern that is repeated in your life, we can look together at why that is so. Why, for example, do you continue to choose partners who are dependent on you and don't give much of themselves when it is so painful for you to do so? Together, we try to figure out when the belief that you need to take care of others in order to be allowed to be present in the world arose.

We go through the feelings like pearls on a string, and when you land in precisely that feeling, I or another healer may ask you: "How old do you feel?" You might answer: "I am very small." Once we have the contact there, we can start meeting the little child, that small part of you for which there hasn't been care, and then you as the adult can begin to heal the overload there has once been. At the same time, you receive help and support in the form of a gentle and tender energy from the spirit world, which heals you both as an adult and as the child you once were.

For example, if we are working in the foetal state, I will go in and connect you with the pillar of light, contact the spirit world and pray that your foetus will be enclosed, as it needs to be so that the transition will be better. Here it will most often be a guardian angel, like Gabriel or one of the others, who is present and works with tenderness and gentleness. When this happens, the alarms that have arisen in the foetal state begin to subside, and, in this way, you are helped to heal the very early responses in the nervous system – either via mother or otherwise – and then you begin to be better at receiving. Back then you had to take in your mother's energy, but now you can start to discriminate and take with you what is good (there is always a deep connection and love between mother and child no matter how much of a mess there may be) and what should be left behind. The foetus begins, so to speak, to repel the negative energy and re-establish a safe nervous system.

THE EXPERIENCE OF FEELING SAFE

The healing supports you in your life today, but also the little child in you. This means that the little child gets the support and care it should have had in order to change a partially frozen state into security, joy and vitality, and the adult you heals so that you have better contact to more of yourself. A lot of the work you do yourself. During healing, you are not your inner child. You are an adult and can become the parent for yourself that you once lacked.

Your inner child is not of course a child that exists in the physical world any more because you have grown up now. But the inner child exists as a consciousness that has been locked into a particular belief, and as a physical response in your nervous system that still exists. Because the experiences of the foetal state or childhood are so deeply embedded, it is difficult for your soul to gain access if there are locked areas or traumas here, and therefore this work can really loosen them up and help you. When you really take care of the little child inside you, it calms down, and so do you. You can say that you are re-teaching the place in yourself that is so small that it can be safe to be here. Thereby your nervous system begins to say, "Oh yes, that's how it is to be safe." The reason it works so strongly is precisely because we go through the nervous system. You develop a greater capacity to love your inner child and your inner child gets an even greater capacity to receive. Suddenly you have the opportunity to choose something that is better for you than what you are used to choosing – for example, a better partner who can also take care of you. You say farewell to something that felt safe because it was familiar but, in reality, was unsafe and bad for you, and you say hello to new, automatic pilots who have a much easier time choosing something good for you. Insecurity locks you and gets you out of yourself. Security expands you, opens you up and gets you to seek both more into yourself and out into the world in a completely different way. All of this becomes possible when we work with our inner child.

FAREWELL TO INSECURITY

It is important to remember that our mental and emotional beliefs, although they may limit us, are there for our survival. Through inner child work, you become aware that there are good reasons why you felt the way you did when you were a foetus, child, or teenager. While it can be painful to look at how it has been, there is no reason to blame yourself, and often not to blame our parents either – they did the best they could. But now you are an adult. The beliefs that have so far kept you alive – actually and figuratively – have fulfilled their purpose, and you can now let go of them and go out into the world in a completely different and freer way, as yourself. When you meet the same atmosphere later in life, you are better able to distinguish between your inner child and your adult self because in the inner child work you go into the atmospheric memory rather than the linguistic or mental one. Maybe you have been strongly rejected as a child, and as an adult it takes almost nothing before you feel rejected and then close off. Through the inner child work, you take hold of your inner little child right where she felt the rejection strongest. When you don't reject her this time but, on the contrary, pick her up, rock her and give her all the love and security she once lacked, she calms down. This has great significance, not just in that moment, but for our entire lives because when we connect with the spirit world and create a connectedness there, a sense of security and access, to peace and clarity arises within us. We also begin to be able to figure out where in the physical world we can experience security, and with which people. It is thus not just about having a sense of security with the spirit world in oneself, but also about the fact that, in your nervous system, there begins to be a sense of security about finding it out in the world. The trauma is healed and you, the adult, can behave differently if you encounter a similar atmosphere again. You can go another way; you have other options.

HARD WORK

Inner child work is effective because we work very precisely at some very deep levels. You can work on it yourself by connecting with the pillar of light and your team of guides and then trying to go through your feelings, mental beliefs or body tensions like pearls on a string – see more about self-healing in Chapter 8. However, it is good to be aware that you must be well established in contact with the spirit world when doing so, otherwise you may experience it as if you were again a small child, lying and reaching up with your arms and no one being there to receive you. This means you will only get confirmation that the world is evil. The team from the spirit world is always there to help you, but if you don't yet have good integration between your body and your soul essence, it may be a good idea to get some help until you can do it yourself. Pain may well be part of self-development, but it isn't healthy for you to be lying alone, struggling in the spider's web. There is no doubt that inner child work can be difficult, but the rewards are correspondingly great. You gain a trust in life when you get your inner child healed and the part of your soul essence for which there was no room for before comes back. Once you gain access to the pure essence within yourself that has been hidden, it can change into a new belief, and you can begin to master something you couldn't do before. Now is the time.

YOUR RELATIONSHIPS, YOUR LIFE

We humans are social beings who are greatly affected by our relationships. The relationships we have with others are also reflected in the way we think about ourselves and the way we treat ourselves.

The early imprints in life are crucial to the pattern we bear with us. It is important to remember that our sensory systems pick up other people and that our systems adapt to those we are with (as I previously wrote about with mirror neurons). The way we enter into relationships is therefore the result of what we have experienced when small and the adaptation or adjustment that has taken place in us. Adaptations are often about survival. As a child, you are completely at the mercy of your surroundings and have to adapt to your closest caregivers physically, emotionally and mentally in order to survive. If early on you are in relationships that aren't healthy – with those that don't connect with you or those who have issues that overwhelm you at a time when you are not ready for it – you may come to take over your mother's pain, your father's powerlessness or the anger of your siblings without you being aware of it. It is simply stored inside you and affects the way you think about yourself. Conversely, good relationships early in life will make you better able to have body contact, presence and access to yourself, so that you make decisions based on your whole being and not simply from "you-as-survivor." Based on healthy relationships, you have access to both your vulnerabilities and your strength, talents and resources.

It is therefore important to keep an eye out for what is a good relationship for you and what is not. Pay attention to how you are feeling in a given relationship when the person is approaching, for example. What happens in you – in your body, your feelings, your thoughts? Do you tense up? Do you become insecure? This can give you a clue as to whether that relationship is good for you or not. It can also be about the person mirroring something in you that has to do with previous relationships. A certain energy, way of being or manner can trigger something from the past. You can also have so much mistrust that you completely shut off from other people under an arrogant and dismissive façade, even if, deep down, you are lonely because previous traumas are being reactivated and patterns are being repeated.

You can thus both be drawn to people who are bad for you, in a repetition of old patterns, and come to reject potentially good relationships due to old traumas. Both of these are inappropriate. The good news is that you can work with it. The inner child work, for example, allows you to go in and heal where the trauma happened, so you don't have to react like a three-year-old every time you have a relationship that reminds you of one you were in when you were that age. Chapter 8 contains a number of exercises that you can carry out yourself, for example, the circle exercise, which is about gaining an overview of the relationships that strengthen you and the relationships that drain you. There is also the bucket exercise and the reverse bucket exercise, which is about giving back to others what isn't yours, and taking back what actually is. Whether you do the exercise one way or the other, the result is that both people in the relationship can be who they are, and can therefore meet healthily. I experienced this, for example, with one of my course participants. She had had an alcoholic mother and had given away a lot of emotional energy to make everyday life work. She was now in her mid-forties. We did a piece of relationship work together, where she let go of old grief and old feelings that she had been carrying for her mother, especially in the area of the liver. We in fact often store these things in our organs, and for her it was especially in the liver. She worked with a very early influence where she had been carrying her mother's weight and problems. Now she let go of it all and gave it over to the healing energy and her mother, which made her experience a great relief and feel better in herself. Shortly afterwards, the mother was hospitalised with cirrhosis and was in bad health. The responsibility had come back to her because she had become ready and had taken her own pain in. The mother stopped drinking and the two have had a good relationship with each other, which has lasted for several years now. Even though the mother is still struggling with her illnesses, such as a small tumour in the liver, her daughter no longer bears the heavy responsibility but can concentrate on herself and her own issues. They reverted to having a good time with each other. Nowadays, for example, they send each other warm messages every day – they appreciate each other from what the daughter calls "a nice place in the heart."

When we are children, the state our parents are in becomes integrated into our bodies, feelings and thoughts. When you as an older person let go of what isn't yours, you get better access to yourself, and the others are allowed to move on in their lives – if they are ready for it. When you work on your early relationships through inner-child healing, you can hold your own ground more when you meet similar people with similar energies or intentions again. You can, so to speak, keep them out of your energy field. That way, the work will help you cope better in relationships or types of relationships that have otherwise taken you out of yourself. You will also be better at assessing which relationships are good for you. Once you have decoded relationships that have created inappropriate reactions in you, you can begin to build good relationships with yourself and the outside world.

When a relationship affects you very intensely, negatively or positively, it can come from previous lives. In this case, you can go in and heal the friction that has been between you in previous lives so that it doesn't repeat itself. Many times, we are born together again to be able to heal and loosen up these blockages in relationships. You can't allow yourself to heal someone who hasn't agreed to it, but you can heal the relationship. Similarly, there may be something in your lineage that makes you react in certain ways to people or relationships – for example, towards authorities, where it is in the lineage to either submit or oppose. See more about this in the chapters on karmic and epigenetic healing.

THE DRAMA TRIANGLE – ARE YOU A PERSECUTOR, A RESCUER OR A VICTIM?

It can be exciting to look at what role you play in a relationship. There is a model called the drama triangle or the victim triangle. It was originally developed in 1968 by Stephen Karpman. The dynamics of the model apply in all kinds of relationships, but are most evident in dysfunctional family and couple relationships. The drama triangle unfolds between three behavioural roles: persecutor, rescuer and victim. The dynamics of the drama triangle arise because the parties involved don't express their wishes honestly and directly. Instead of taking responsibility for their feelings, those involved begin a game of social manipulation to get their needs satisfied.

Most often, people don't take on just one role; we occupy them all. When the rescuer feels like a victim, he switches to persecutor and gets surly and angry. So the persecutor always has some sadness and loneliness in the background, which also needs to be recognised. The victim is waiting to be rescued, but can't act of his own accord to change the situation – he or she, like a young cuckoo, doesn't possess the courage to fly out of the nest and live his/her own life. A victim can be passive or an aggressive energy who grumbles until someone comes along and rescues them.

The drama triangle is an unhealthy pattern. The rescuer isn't herself rescued, the persecutor pushes everyone away and the victim finishes up in a passive state and is unable to do anything about it. Everything goes wrong. There is nothing to be gained by being in this pattern, and yet it is very normal in many relationships. You can have the same drama triangle within you, that is, in your relationship with yourself; it is just as destructive. If you notice that in your outer or inner relationships you are trapped in the patterns of the drama triangle, then try looking at what really lies beneath the role you are taking on. Is it loneliness? An unmet need? An old anxiety? The better you are in touch with yourself, the clearer you can stand your ground towards others. Also, look at when you fall into the pattern; what do you really need to express? We have access to feel it when we have access to our soul essences; here you rest in yourself and step outside the persecutor-rescuer-victim triangle. So when you have access to your soul essence, you can stand your ground much better.

Once you start recognising when you get into these roles, you can start working on what gets you into them. You can go in search of the early imprints that are no longer appropriate for you. What situations did they arise in? When did it start? You can heal the traumas that lie in the background, so that you don't have to go into them.

HARD TO LET GO

You may find it difficult to let go of other people's feelings and moods. You can be held in their grip by fear or guilt, and the result is that it is negative atmospheres that keep you together, rather than love bonds, where there is an atmosphere of energy exchange with flexibility. It is understandable that you may be scared, but you have everything to gain by continuing with the relationship work. When you are working with external relationships, you are also working with your internal relationships. You work with the voice of your parents or your teachers telling you that you aren't good enough. Or the feeling that there is too much to deal with, so that everything becomes impossible and unmanageable. Your old patterns sit in all your cells and get in the way of you living and creating. The way to heal them involves self-care, feeling your essence and radiating into the world as who you are.

TAKE RESPONSIBILITY

When we work with relationships, it is important to remember that we don't only take on other people's stuff, but can also project our own unprocessed stuff into others. A projection is a psychological defence mechanism that involves transferring one's own problematic feelings, perceptions or characteristics to other people or relationships. Just as you are a sponge to the outside world, the outside world is a sponge to you. It can therefore be a good idea to take back your energy so that you take responsibility instead of passing it on to others. You may have been aggressive instead of showing that you were upset, or you may have shut off and become cold instead of showing that you were insecure. Now it is lying out there somewhere, like garbage that hasn't been collected. Other people may be walking around with issues of which they don't know the origin and you yourself may be having a hard time healing completely because you are missing a part of yourself.

Those people to whom we are closest – our children, parents, partner or work colleagues – are often the ones we subject to this behaviour. Take back your energy and ask for healing. Consciously or unconsciously, you have passed it on to others because there was something to which you couldn't relate. When you take back that energy, both you and the other become more balanced. The reverse bucket exercise, which I describe in Chapter 8, can be a great help with this.

TAKE RESPONSIBILITY FOR YOUR PART
CONSCIOUSLY AND UNCONSCIOUSLY

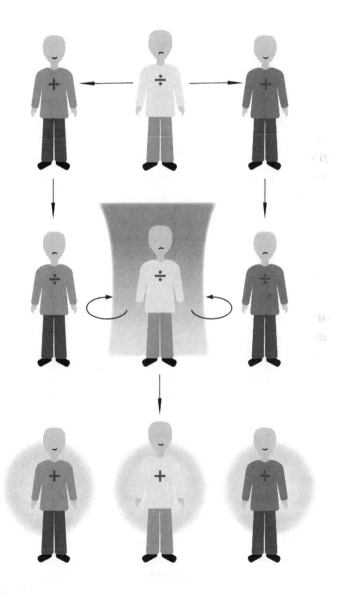

***

Mette's story:
'I HAVE FOUND PEACE WITH WHAT I
BROUGHT WITH ME.'

Mette was born prematurely as the child of two very young people, each of whom lacked love and security in their upbringings. Out of this came a small human being with a great sensitivity towards others. Through inner child work on several levels, Mette, who is now 51 years old, has found a way to be comfortable with what is and what was; she completed a healing journey where she had full attention on the needs of her inner child, which are going to continue for all eternity, she says.

"Inner-child work is our constant companion when we work with ourselves. After all, our inner children are with us throughout life, even when we are teenagers, adults, middle-aged and older. The inner child is, if you will, the basic food parcel we received from our parents and our lineage, that which we never chose ourselves but with which we have to deal.

I have often had the feeling that if I had also been given a small water bottle, a warm blanket and some good hiking shoes in the 'food parcel,' then perhaps I would have gone out into the world in a different, healthier way. Then it might have been possible for me to be myself much earlier in life. Since this wasn't possible for a long time, there is a lot of powerlessness, sadness, anger and frustration in me and in my little inner child. As much as it is possible, I can now heal and change the content in relation to taste and needs, and it is great that the food parcel is increasingly becoming my own and not just one I got handed out to me. With those opportunities and those changes, pleasure begins to turn up in my life.

Mette's food parcel

I am the product of two very young parents who each in their own way have lacked love and security. My mother loses her mother when she is 13 years old, and her father, who may always have been absent, becomes even more absent at that point. She isn't taken care of, and the loss of her mother isn't addressed. She doesn't get the feeling of being cared for physically and psychologically and grows up with a feeling of insecurity as her companion. Because of this, a deep longing to start a family and become WHOLE arises in her. My father comes from a large family, where nobody showed or talked about their feelings. Instead of love, there are slaps, and here too it is important to grow up quickly and get away from the dysfunctional family life. The two emotionally immature and damaged young people are no more than 19 years old when they have me. They have no control over their lives, themselves or each other.

I am born five and a half weeks premature. The contractions start, and even though my mother, contrary to all custom at the time, has insisted on my father being present at the birth, he is sent home again, because I am not due yet. They keep my mother in for observation, but the birth begins, and she ends up giving birth alone in abandonment and powerlessness. When I am born, I am not even allowed to come up to be with her but taken, put in an incubator and transported away. I am moved to the Children's Hospital, where I lie in a ward with a lot of other children in incubators, as was the practice with premature babies at the time. The parents weren't allowed to come in to their children, pick them up or hold them. They had to content themselves with standing on the other side of a window, looking in at their child. Here we small infants lie, regulating ourselves according to the surroundings – in this case to each other. It has been insecure and unbearable, and I learn early on to have the attention on everyone else but myself because I have to find some kind of security somewhere out there. What an atmosphere and energy there must have been in such a ward. So I lie there without close contact with my parents and their security and love, together with other premature babies who are just as insecure and abandoned as I am. I am not breastfed but fed by bottle and I have a feeling we are being routinely handled instead of being held.

Outside, on the other side of the window, stands my mother, crying, a young woman without support who can't be with her child, and who is greeted by the staff with 'then you'd better go home if it makes you so sad.' She has to pull herself together – and so do I, on the other side of the window. My father is no support; he just gets angry at my mother when she cries.

When he doesn't have room for her feelings, she gets the feeling of being abandoned.

I'm sure my dad also feels powerless and is finding it difficult. He isn't a 'cold' person, but he hasn't been brought up to put an arm around others, comfort them and support them, so he is unable to accommodate her and all the feelings she has. They are both alone with their feelings, just as I am with mine. We are all in a state of powerlessness and abandonment, with a glass pane between us.

Insecure and rebellious

I have been smothered in all this from the moment I started my life, so it soon becomes a challenge to separate what is mine and what is someone else's. As a child you just want to know that you are wanted and loved, but my parents are so young and have such a need for love and security themselves that that weighs heavier than giving me what I need. They are simply unable.

My Dad and Mum get divorced when I'm one and a half years old, and my Dad gets married again when I'm two years old to a woman who doesn't want me to be there. She is nice enough, but not happy that I'm there because I am an unwanted symbol of my father's past without her. At my Mum's, there are changing boyfriends. She still wants to have a family. I am born into insecurity, and I continue to be insecure – no fixed framework and no fixed structure. Because that insecurity lies so deep inside me, I can already, as a child, automatically and naturally feel the insecurity and uneasiness in others. I quickly become a human 'heat cannon' who goes in and warms up and listens when others are having a hard time. Something in me simply starts automatically in an intense desire to heal what I feel the other person needs. Every time I do it, it feels a little better inside me. At school I am often used for taking care of the 'weak ones,' calming the 'aggressive ones' and comforting those who are sad. Unconsciously, I feel and understand what they are feeling inside. They register that, and the healing starts.

In my teens, I become extroverted and rebellious. I wear too much make-up, date too many boys and go into town when I am too young – all to find some kind of confirmation so I can feel safe. I have a feeling that other people don't like me, even if it isn't true.

I feel a discomfort when I am with other people; I just don't know that it is their discomfort that I am feeling. It makes it hard for me to let others in, even if they want to be with me. To get in to me, you first have to defeat dragons and get past cannons, and many give up long before that.

There is a basic feeling within me of not being good enough and worth loving. In relationships I am often the one who pulls out first, either because I don't feel loved and respected as who I am or as a self-destructive protection of myself. When female friends compete with me on being popular with the boys or having the most good points, I recognise the element of competition from several layers in my life, including from having half-siblings, where I am always the loser, the one without a mother and father to live with, and I can't cope with that. I get scared and insecure when someone indicates that they like me, because I am not familiar with that, and I would rather be safe than sorry.

A crucial meeting

However, when I meet my future husband, something new happens. We meet when I am only 16, but the relationship ends because the maturity isn't really there yet. So I find an older boyfriend and move away from home as a 17-year-old. With him there is a basic feeling but not a real falling-in-love. When I meet my current husband again in town two years later, we can both feel that there is 'something' and I go straight home and break up with my boyfriend. In my husband, I find what I have never had: a safe anchor. When I look into his eyes, I get the feeling of coming HOME. I can find the place that feels like 'home,' in and with him – something in me allows itself to open up in safety and security, and I dare to reach out, ask him to say he loves me, ask to hold me and let me sit on his lap. You could say that I break the vicious circle that has started much further back in my lineage than with me. Or at least, I make a start on it, because I am still struggling with it to this day, and of course we have had a lot to work with through a long life together. I know that we love each other and will always work things out – we have decided that!

We have three children together and they are all born prematurely, just like me. By taking care of them during the weeks and months when they are admitted to neonatal wards, it is as if I get the opportunity to rewrite the story and heal my own inner child. For example, when my eldest daughter is born prematurely, I insist, right after the birth, that my husband goes with her as they put her in an incubator in another ward — she just mustn't be alone. It triggers my sense of abandonment, and I know how important it is that she doesn't get the feeling of being abandoned. My twins are born even more prematurely than me, but the conditions are different because, by now, parents are allowed to be with their children in hospitals. They are held, laid on our bare bellies and breasts and are allowed to lie together in the same incubator – they are never alone. So subconsciously I get to take care of my own inner child by giving my children other opportunities for a start in life. I act differently from my parents, psychologically, physically and mentally.

Reaching out to grandma

In 2005, I get cancer, and while I am hospitalised and lying there scared, I reach out to my beloved paternal grandmother, who died two years before. A little while after, a nurse who introduces herself as Solveig – the same name that my grandmother had – comes into the ward. Before then, I had never reached out to the spirit world in that way. I have known that it was there and that there was something more, but I had a feeling that it was separate from me. The illness becomes a trigger for me to investigate and work with my own spiritual side. At that time, I have already had a smouldering feeling for a while of lacking something more: that I need more than just children, husband and work. So I start taking courses in clairvoyance, healing and being a medium. My inner child is involved in it all, because there is a scared little girl, who doesn't dare to be visible and doesn't dare to unfold herself for fear of being rejected or weighed up and found too lightweight.

For me, the spirit world is many things. There is the Presence of God, who loves us unconditionally, and the 'Light of the Universe,' which is more loving, pure, and true than we are. When we can connect with it, it is truly healing for the little child's nervous system; we feel safe, embraced, cared for and completely relaxed – in this luminous embrace, we can be ourselves as we were and are.

Being in the presence of deceased relatives is also truly healing. When a person we love passes away, we can continue to have them with us in our lives in a different way and feel that they are holding their hand over us or following us, just like my grandmother did to me.

I can always get the help in the spirit world that I can't always get in the earthly world. Even though my husband is 'home' for me, we can also be on such bad terms that it isn't possible to feel at home right then and there. In those cases where I feel lost and without a foothold, I can always connect with Grandma, God, the pillar of light or just the spirit world. Then I will feel safe and can find a foothold. Then I can also more easily get out of the state where I stand and stomp like a little child and say, 'You must love me!' because there is always love to be found in the spirit world – I just have to reach out and I will be taken care of.

Now my mother can hear me
I am my inner child, my inner child is me, and my food parcel will always be the one I brought with me. So my work continues to direct my attention towards, and take care of, little Mette. I am aware of what the blockages and shortcomings of my lineage are and that they are not mine. In those cases, healing and attention are the best ways of changing old, inherited patterns. When we heal blockages in the lineage, there is space for the good, resource-filled

currents to be allowed to fill our lives – what comes out of it is always exciting. I have got much more peace. I know I can take care of myself so I no longer require others to do it. I still want them to do it, but I'm not dependent on it, and it brings peace to my relationships. Sometimes I reach out to the spirit world, and other times to a human being, my husband, for example. I can say, 'May I sit on your lap?' from the little place in me that is needy. He can do it and I will be received where I wasn't received before. It is magical when it happens and can be done.

All in all, that means I have been able to release my anger towards my parents. I understand them better and understand where they have come from and what their circumstances were. I have been so incredibly angry at them: at my father because he couldn't show or say that he loves me and at my mother because her longing and abandonment took precedence over mine. After all, it was me who was the child! It should have been them who took care of me, for it must always be the parents who take care of the children, and not the other way round. But when they couldn't do that, it was good that I had tools to use. The relationship between the inner child and the parents is reflected in all relationships, so it means a lot in many contexts that I have healed my relationship with them. Today I can accept what they can give me, because I am now in a more secure place with myself. I won't be trading blows any more. For many years, I couldn't cope with having a relationship with them; I could almost get claustrophobic if I got a text message or a phone call. Today, I can enjoy what is without being preoccupied with what should have been.

I recently had a talk with my mother about all this, and although I think I have told her about it many times before in the most honest and vulnerable way, she actually said to me: 'Now I can hear what you're saying.' I don't think I put it any differently, but my aura and energy were new; an energy that didn't lock her in a feeling of inadequacy, but allowed her to relax and feel good enough with who she is. Even though I haven't said it in words, today I express that: 'I can take care of myself now, but I still need a mother.' Hopefully I have broken the circle in my relationship with my own children. Probably not all of it because we are just human beings after all, but if there is another foundation that is as it should be, there is always to which something they can hold on."

***

Endnotes

5   Locked areas and traumas can also originate from your lineage (epigenetic) or your soul (karmic), as we shall see in the next chapters. Here we are looking at the life you have lived since you were conceived and your soul was beginning to collaborate with your new body.

6   Endnote: As a healer, I always look for who comes down when I am working with a client. Are they angels, guides, creatures from nature or the dead? That tells me something about who the person orientates themselves towards and therefore will benefit from getting in closer contact with.

CHAPTER 5 – in brief

- Your childhood has a big impact on how you integrate your soul essence and, thereby, what themes and challenges you have with you later in life. The locked areas or trauma comes about at a certain time, and when we know this time, we can work very precisely with healing.

- Overall, childhood can be divided into four periods, where certain things happen in the development of our brains and bodies, which can trigger certain problems. The four periods are: the foetal state to 1 year; 2 to 5 years; 6 to 12 years, and the teens.
- The first period includes themes such as overactive or balanced nervous systems, over-responsibility, sensitivity, security, abandonment, being accepted and physical boundaries. The second includes themes that are about love and daring to open up to it, as well as the age of defiance and boundaries. The third includes mental development, emotional contact, soul contact and social relationships outside the home. The fourth again includes boundaries, heart opening and identity. This doesn't mean that themes such as these can only belong to specific periods, just that they are typical of these periods.
- When we work with the inner child through healing, we go through the feelings like pearls on a string and try to work out the part of childhood to which they belong. We ask for support from the spirit world, as it comes and heals both you – the adult – and your inner child. You are thus not the little child during the healing. You are the adult who is taking care of the little child.
- Through working on your inner child, you can put aside the survival strategies that were once crucial, and live more freely and in accordance with your soul essence.
- You can work with your inner child alone, but make sure you are well-integrated so that you do not traumatise yourself again. Always remember to get in touch with the necessary blockages and insights at the time you are ready.

**AT MARZCIA.DK YOU CAN
FIND THESE MEDITATIONS:**

Bucket exercise
(described in chapter 8)

Healing of foetus

Relationship with Mother

Relationship with Father

Healing of relationships with others

CHAPTER 6

THERE IS HELP IN YOUR LINEAGE

About epigenetic healing

Have you ever had the feeling that you could suddenly smell your grandmother's Chloé perfume or a hint of the smoke from your grandfather's old cheroots? And have you become happy and secure in the memory of their loving support or, conversely, frightened and afraid because it has been a long time since they left you here on Earth? I hope the first one applies to you, but I know at the same time that such an experience may well be frightening for some people if they don't know that their deceased relative is most often just eager to help; it applies no matter how the relationship has been while they were alive. Actually, complicated relationships are often easier to deal with when the person is dead and the weight of earthly life is no longer a disturbance. You can therefore easily experience that a person with whom you had a hard time or who was distant for you while he or she was alive comes back to help you, now full of eagerness and desire. You can also get visits from relatives you don't know or those from far back in your lineage, and it can be a great liberation not just for you but also for them.

OUR ANCESTORS HAVE ALWAYS HELPED

For millennia, man has sought the help of ancestors for life here on Earth, and in some societies it is still quite common. This is true of Hawaii, for example, where I have been taught by a wonderful healer, Sean Keahi. For him, asking the ancestors for advice is only natural. It isn't even something he gives a second thought as a medium. He just has a deep connection into his lineage and a knowledge that his relatives always come and give support, both in his own life and when he performs healing work. In the tradition from which he comes, the ancestors count not only humans but also the trees, the turtles and the other creatures in the water. There is a deep contact with nature, souls and consciousnesses – and also a responsibility. Because, as Sean says, "We are the crown jewels. We have survived because our lineage has been strong. Our task is thus to carry the lineage forward in the best possible way in relation to the life we live, the society we live in and the people we are."

That was also the case in our culture at one time. But as we in the Western world have separated the soul from science and become far less spiritual in general, we have also come further away from the support and help that lies in our lineage, which is a real shame, because potentially, there are not only a lot of old blockages and traumas lying in the our lineage, which create problems to this day, but also solutions to the very same problems and, above all, help that we shouldn't be without. The lineage is our foundation, our heritage and our solution. You know it when you look in the mirror and recognise your grandfather's brown eyes or your mother's shy smile: you are your lineage deep into your cells, but that doesn't mean you are at the mercy of everything that comes from your lineage. Put in a biological way: it isn't inevitable that you express all your genes in a particular way. You can change your life, your physique and your mind. You can even change the way your lineage develops and, so to speak, break the social epigenetic legacy. This means that there is really a lot you can do yourself for the benefit of both you and your lineage.

In this chapter, I want to tell you about what epigenetic healing is and how I use it in my practice. My hope is that it will inspire you to seek help in your lineage – and maybe even help your lineage. There is so much love, support and development to be found!

VISITS DURING HEALING – HEALING DURING VISITS

I came to work with epigenetic healing for two reasons. One was that when I was healing clients, I quite often saw a deceased person come forward and help me with the healing. It could be a dear grandfather that my client had been missing. Because of the grief and loss, she had closed her heart. Because the client's sensory apparatus was now open during the healing, she was able to open her heart again and relive the love, to sense and sometimes recognise her relative. Perhaps the client didn't discover that it was her grandfather who had come during the healing, but subconsciously, his presence was there and did healing on her grief so that the good memories and the new or rediscovered presence could emerge and she could open up to the world again. Sometimes I said to the client, "I got the sense it was your grandfather. He said that…" Other times I just let it happen. It wasn't so central; the important thing was that a healing process started. Sometimes the wounds healed are quite intense. A client might have come and had major problems with an alcoholic parent, where there had been a lot of pain, violation, abuse and betrayal. Now this parent, who was dead and therefore free of mental and physical bonds and closer to his own soul essence than ever came through, and was ready to take responsibility. If, for example, it was an alcoholic father, he could now take the negative energy with which he had influenced his child, and which the child had been carrying around, and say: "Now I am ready to carry it myself." In that way, he could let the very precise love flow instead, the love which is always present from a parent to a child but which he had had difficulty expressing. This could again happen consciously, by probing the client about what they experienced: "Does it make sense that your father had these issues?" Other times it could come up afterwards when I wake the client up and ask what had happened during the healing. Then she might answer, "I had all these unpleasant pictures of my father, but suddenly I got a glimpse of loving experiences." Because her system, her thoughts and feelings had been healed, there was suddenly room to notice where there had been glimpses of love between her and her father too. This contact between the living and the deceased can help create a new beginning and a better basis for closeness between father and daughter. Other times there may be grief over having lost a very close, loving relative, and when the deceased then comes and lends support, the grief can ease and the heart contact and the closeness can be re-established to the great joy of both the living and the deceased. For many years, I just noticed that this was happening without really developing it further. I just opened up and let those who wanted to come along do a piece of work when I was healing.

At the same time – and this was the second reason why I began to work with epigenetic healing – I discovered that when I had deceased contacts with an audience, something similar happened. A deep healing took place when the deceased relatives came with care and messages for the living. I could feel the love and see the transformation that happened within my audience and that the recipients also expressed. It became increasingly clear to me how important such a meeting could be and also that there were many deceased people who wanted to get in touch once I opened the lock gates. I actually had to pay a little attention, especially when there was a person in my audience whose deceased relative was finding it easy to come through – the ones I today call "deceased magnets." Once the deceased mother has come through, then the maternal grandmother, the father and the rest of the family are there as well, and then it can quickly end up with no one else in the audience getting messages that night. I sense far more deceased relatives than I can manage to facilitate on such an evening. I could quickly be standing there with one thousand deceased relatives to an audience of two hundred! And they all want to reach their living relatives at the same time the living want contact with their deceased. Contacts, healing and support also often come to the audience members I don't manage to notify because their deceased relatives are around them all evening.

The deceased relatives came of their own accord when I was healing, and when I was acting as a medium, a healing happened, so I began engaging with it more purposefully.

FAMILY CONSTELLATIONS WITH REAL RELATIVES

One theorist I have been inspired by in epigenetic work is the German priest and psychotherapist Bert Hellinger (1925–2019), who developed the family therapy form Family Constellations. In its basic form, it means that, with the help of "extras," you place your family in a specific constellation in order to create an overview of the family dynamics and the main character – i.e., the client – in relation to the other family members. The client thereby tries to investigate some themes in themselves, which may originate from the family. She might want to find out why she is suffering from anxiety. She stands in the middle and looks at her "family," and with the therapist as facilitator, she and the extras play through some situations between her and her family, which makes the interaction visible and specific and allows her to break the patterns and perhaps get rid of her anxiety.

I talked to people who have taken part in Family Constellations sessions who have been able to tell me that they in fact not only played a mother or an aunt, but could also feel the presence of the dead person they were playing – some even had difficulty in getting rid of this contact with the deceased again because they weren't trained in opening and closing access to the deceased plane. From these stories, I discovered that there was great potential in working with deceased relatives, such that it was not "just" someone who played Aunt Ida in Family Constellations, but that it really was her. It makes a big difference to how strong a healing can come through to the living and in fact also to the lineage. When I train my epigenetic healing students, they do an exercise where one of them has a desire for the healing of a theme of an epigenetic nature. Two other students with abilities in contact with deceased people get in touch with the respective relatives of the living person. The two students now convey the deceased person's story, their intention of lending support and their responsibility for the theme with which their living relatives struggle, whereby intense healing takes place. It is a really good exercise to illustrate what happens in epigenetic healing, although the healer doesn't always get the deceased's story quite so directly.

UNHAPPY LOVE IN YOUR GENES

The Family Constellations method makes a lot of sense to me and it is a great inspiration in my work. However, I carry out my epigenetic healing in a slightly different way. I begin by very specifically asking the relatives who have something constructive to contribute to step forward. When I do that, more people are happy to come forward than the usual one or two who would come under a regular healing. Many times, some deceased relatives emerge who are the reason for the theme with which the client is struggling. For example, it could be that you come to me as a client because you have a big problem with bad relationships. Now, during the healing, a deceased relative who has experienced not being able to get the one he or she really loved arrives. In the old days, it was sometimes difficult to be allowed to have the one you loved because you were part of different hierarchies. The farmer's son was under no circumstances allowed to fall in love with the countess's daughter, but it still happened all the time, most often with very unhappy endings. Perhaps there has been such an unhappy story in your family, and it has led to distrust in your family towards love – a distrust in love being able to succeed, you could say.

That distrust lies in the genetic structure you carry with you from your lineage; it lies in your mental and emotional beliefs. But you can break the vicious circle. In order to understand how, we need to take a little tour around genetics and cell biology; we will get back to the unfulfilled love again!

EPIGENETICS: THE WAY YOUR GENES EXPRESS THEMSELVES

Epigenetics actually means "besides genetics." Epigenetic research deals with how the genes we carry with us express themselves. It doesn't mean that because we have a specific gene, something specific will always be expressed in us. You may have a gene for a disease or a trait without developing it. Many different factors can influence how our genes express themselves and whether, for example, we develop a number of mental illnesses – whether the gene we carry for it is activated. Unpleasant experiences, drugs and stress are some of the factors that affect whether a gene is expressed. Conversely, good experiences, presence and a healthy environment can prevent a gene from being expressed. The American cell biologist Bruce Lipton has developed theories about how cells are not only susceptible to physical factors in their environment, but also by our mental consciousness and emotional states. In his principal work, *The Biology of Belief,*[7] he explains how, after the downer of his life with divorce and the loss of his researcher title, he went and lived in the Caribbean for a year and completely changed his view of his life as a human being and his views as a cell biologist. In the book, it becomes clear that it isn't the DNA in our cell nuclei that determines which genes are active but, to a much greater degree, which surrounding environment is affecting the cells. Genes are activated or deactivated according to what the cell membranes allow into the cell nucleus. In its essence, it is about the fact that we aren't at the mercy of our genes, but can work with what we have inherited and play a part in changing that inheritance. This offers very great potential for the epigenetic healing processes. Because of a change in the environment of the cells from stress-influenced to rest- or security-influenced, a change in gene expression occurs when our nervous system shifts from a sympathetic stress response to a parasympathetic response of relaxation, regeneration and security. Joy creates different gene activations from, for example, grief. This means that there is a strong connection between your moods and thoughts and how your genes express themselves. A healing from a deceased relative, who has facilitated gene expressions that repeat depressed states, can thus help a lot.

EPIGENETIC HEALING

HEAL YOUR LINEAGE

And now back to the unfulfilled love. The genes you are carrying all the way from your relative, the farmer's son, who wasn't allowed to have the countess's daughter, are still in you today. Even if you aren't in the same situation or living in the same society as him, you may have challenges with love and feel that no matter what you do, you will never get the one you love. You could say that it sounds a little simplistic that you have several gene activations that result in miserable couple relationships. Unfulfilled love simply comes around again, relative by relative. But now you are ready to get rid of the theme; you are tired of bad relationships and want to be loved and cared for. Your willingness to work with it means that your lineage has evolved and is able to evolve further. You have a greater chance of breaking the theme than your 16th-century relative. And the wonderful thing is that when you do, it also heals the person who had the pain to begin with, that is, your deceased relative. He is given the opportunity to take responsibility for his pain, relate to it and heal it. For you as a living person, this means that you can drop something you have been carrying that has been in your family. By doing so, there will also be room for the relatives who have actually experienced good relationships to have a better opportunity to provide healing and support to you. The genes that have to do with good relationships and being able to give and receive love are activated. You discover that you not only have genes for unfulfilled love, but also for success in a good love relationship. In this way, it becomes not only a healing of a trauma, but also a positive help from the "good" deceased. You have relatives who can support you positively in activating the good genes for love, and you have the farmer's son, who has experienced the trauma and has activated the genes where it has not succeeded. The genes of the farmer's son can be deactivated. You can thereby regain the feeling of opening your heart and becoming safe and seeking good relationships. In other words, you can finally have a happy love relationship.

From being bound to a trauma in your family, you gain access to a greater part of your soul essence and a quality that lies in your genes for happiness. You experience that you become more loving, open and present. In this way, your relatives who have had the problem back in time (the farmer's son), yourself in your present and your family in the future are all healed both because you aren't passing on the bad theme yourself and because your relatives' incarnations are now healed. Many of them are already living their lives again, here on Earth or somewhere else. Thus, when the deceased relative and you start working together, it may very well be that he or she has a part of his or her soul reborn as your child or your sister's son or a third, completely separate constellation close to you. We are often in the same types of constellations many times. And when the epigenetic healing begins the negative bond between you and the relative becomes a strong, positive connection. It heals not only the deceased relative, but also the living person who has a part of your relative's soul incarnated.[8] Then a living person may suddenly feel that something loosens and they have an easier time with some things – completely without knowing why.

Whilst the farmer's son in the 16th century was at the mercy of some circumstances that might have made his attitude towards love a good survival mechanism, you aren't at the mercy of the same conditions. You could say that if your problem, for example with love, is epigenetic, then it has helped your lineage to survive. The old theme is thus not something out of which you should berate and fight your way, but something you should lovingly and tenderly let go. The distrust of romantic love has been necessary at a time when it has ensured that your ancestor married befitting his rank in society and could carry on your lineage. You can be grateful and loving for that. But now you may let go of that distrust because the circumstances have changed and your lineage has evolved. Now it is your turn to love.

You can thus help to break a negative epigenetic legacy and instead build on the good qualities that are also in your family.

Remember that if your lineage hadn't been strong, then you wouldn't have been here today. There is always something good on which to continue building.

WHEN GRANDMA ISN'T READY

Not all deceased people are ready to work on their themes. Just as you yourself may be prepared or not prepared on different planes, the deceased experience a similar phenomenon. But if you are ready, then the relatives who are ready to work turn up. You can also help the deceased who isn't quite ready yet by simply getting started working on the theme. Perhaps your grandmother had a theme that was about not realising her potential. She lived in a time when it was difficult for women to get an education and use their intelligence in a job, and that meant she became a bitter woman who inflicted guilt on others. You can now begin to see if you have your grandmother's bitterness in you and begin to heal it. Even though your grandmother may not be ready, by starting to heal that theme, you can create an energy that releases it, perhaps with the help of others in the family. With assistance from your efforts, there is a wave of energy that hits her so that she gets moving, and then a lot can happen. She may be able to get so much energy added that she can get it released. Maybe the theme started much further back with a different ancestor who is ready to come forward. He or she is now hit by the wave as it loosens the trauma. In this way, you again help to heal both backwards and forwards in your family because you yourself are ready. If she isn't ready, there will be others from your lineage who are. And suddenly there is a surplus energy that means that she can be ready. You can see it a bit like healing waves of light travelling through, both backwards in the lineage and forwards.

DON'T YOU FIT IN?

Some of my students and clients experience that they are born into families where they feel very different from the others in the living family. Here it can be a tremendous support to find someone in the family with whom you have similarities. While healing, I will always ask that those who are best right now to support the person or people I am healing come forward. I can also specifically ask for help from those who have some similarities with the client. When I guide epigenetic healing meditations, the students occasionally have an experience of some relatives who have similarities with the student emerging with luminous torches down through all the generations. It isn't really torches but rather their soul essences that light up to show that there is recognition and support for the living relative. It gives tremendous power to experience that recognition – that there is actually someone in our lineage who can do the same things we do, who has the same potential. After all, we share DNA with our family, so it makes sense that there are others who have the same potential we do. Some may even help us to bring out in us what has been under-represented due to limitations of the present life: family contexts or societal contexts where it hasn't been possible to get support, stimulation or acceptance for those certain qualities. If you become connected to some relatives who have that access, you are more likely to be able to use your abilities because you can lean on someone who actually knows them. In our lived lives, we often use our biological family, friends, or perhaps a good teacher for the same thing. The feeling isn't much different when deceased relatives help us. The feeling is of support from a loved one who has a deeper understanding of what you contain. That experience alone makes a big difference to self-confidence. You can look at it as a major expansion of your circle of people who are resources; rather than being limited by the few that are around you here and now, you can involve all of your former relatives for help and support.

A SCIENTIST, A HEALER – OR AN ACCOUNTANT!

Our lineage doesn't only carry blockages and negative patterns. We can also find support in our lineage for all the good things we want and are. Many of those we in the spirit world call guides are actually, I believe, our relatives who come and help us. For example, I have some guides I have used when doing my research, and I am sure I have some scientists behind me in my lineage. Otherwise, I wouldn't have had that fire in me to examine and understand. I am also pretty sure I have a strong team of spiritual beings behind me who have been working with healing and guidance. I have a strong feeling that there are some very old relatives behind me who have worked on these things and who can help me regain knowledge that we have lost in the last few centuries where we have had such a strong focus on science.

In the lineage, there is also help for what we don't express so well. My grandfather was an accountant, for example, and I'm not very good at numbers. I therefore asked my grandfather for help with that part of my business. He has taken it very literally. When my assistant recently had to take over my accounts because I was on sick leave, she suddenly said, "Oh, how cold it has become in here. I don't understand it. It was simply so warm just now." Just at that moment, my grandfather came by because we were sitting with the accounts. It gives me peace of mind to know that I don't have to be in control of everything. My grandfather will surely help me get the right ones to help me – like my assistant.

OUR CONNECTEDNESS AS HUMAN BEINGS

In epigenetic healing, our genetic material is supported to once again be the best possible version through which our soul essences can work. If we have too many blockages, the soul essence can't work so well in the lived, physical life. The cooperation in the family also lies in the desire for us to succeed because if we succeed, so too does the lineage. If we now raise this one level up, then we are all connected as a species, as humanity. Therefore epigenetic healing is a way of resolving the bonds and conflicts that are bound to lineages and physical places. Clearly, there is a liberation happening around humanity. When a single person is ready to say yes to a process that lies in the lineage, the lineage gives support, and the healing process begins; then a greater unity arises, which really creates a great liberation for the individual, for the lineage and for humanity as a whole. There are so many scars and wounds in our common, human history that we need to heal, and epigenetic healing is a powerful remedy for this. My feeling is that right now we need it to go a little faster than it has been going so far. We need to become a united humanity soon to combat the global difficulties we face – for example, the climate catastrophe. The corona crisis showed us that we are interdependent globally and that cooperation is possible, both between individuals and between countries and continents. I hope we don't need equally violent reversals to take matters seriously and take responsibility. That is, of course, a very faint hope. But the more attention there is on how much we affect each other with our emotions, thoughts and actions, the better we can support and understand each other. We are connected as human beings, karmically and epigenetically, and if we have some problematic themes, resolving them is crucial for us. Life isn't just about the individual; our themes will automatically affect others like rings spreading in the water: in this life, in past lives and in the next ones.

HAWAII AND THE PHYSICAL CONNECTION

Epigenetic healing thus has huge potential – for you, your family and humanity. Perhaps there is also potential in relation to physical illnesses. When there is healing, I definitely see less stress and restlessness in the heart, and the question then is whether it is a mental or physical effect. I have also noticed that epigenetic healing, to an even greater degree than the others, helps to manifest the soul essence on a physical level, into the physical life, because it is more closely connected with the physical body and with our DNA and the life of the lineage on Earth.

My Hawaiian healing teacher Sean Keahi has trained me in Lomi Lomi, a physical form of healing massage that helps with physical, mental and emotional tension and pain. His healing massage makes the client's soul essence and energy system work really well with the body. This goes so well with my own basic philosophy that you need to be in balance on all planes to be whole. It isn't enough for it only to be in the soul plane. For me, things form a synthesis when the lineage helps us get our whole system to cooperate within ourselves and with the world. With Sean, I experience an authentic, original way of being in touch with the divine or the spirit world: a natural matter of course, which is so far from what we have here in Denmark. Sean and I do a lot of the same things; when he begins a healing, he enters into a prayer where he asks God and the relatives to be present. This is equivalent to the way I always start by opening myself to healing and asking all those from the spirit world who have something constructive to contribute to step forward. It isn't that Sean has taught me to heal, but he has retaught me something that my ancestors used until we separated soul and body and spirituality from our lives. I am sure his way of doing it is reminiscent of the way we have done it before in our culture.

Sean thinks I am poor because I don't know my family very far back. He himself knows his and his wife's families many generations back. He has taken me to several holy places with really powerful energy, and we visited his wife's family's consecrated ground for their deceased relatives, which is also a sacred place to contact the ancestors and tell the very old family legends. I have had some very touching experiences, sensing the strong contact they have with their relatives and the oneness and strength it gives the family. It has definitely given me a longing to have the same knowledge and contact with my own lineage; the sense of belonging that is far more than the time I am living in and the few generations I know of. Such an anchoring gives a completely different basic feeling of both strength and gratefulness because we stand on the shoulders of some of those who have fought for us to be able to live today. Sean has given me the task of finding out more about my family, simply because there is so much support and help there. The more knowledge you have about your lineage, the easier it is for you to connect with it.

SUPPORT FROM OTHER LINEAGES

While it is mainly your mother's and father's lineages that matter to your DNA and your epigenetic activations, there may in fact be other lineages that support you and your family. In epigenetic healing, other lineages often come in and give a little extra so that you can get the best out of everything you contain from your own lineage.

Personally, I often feel support from Jette's lineage. When I had my first recording for the TV show *The Spirits Return*, I visited a family where there was a great deal of spiritual activity. In the kitchen, for example, things were being moved around in the cupboards. When I stood there in the kitchen and sensed the deceased lady, I was shown an old copy of Miss Jensen's Cookbook, which Jette's father's aunt had used. We have it at home with her handwritten notes in it. Amalie, as this aunt was called, was a bit of a live wire and I have heard many stories about her and felt her presence plenty of times. Right here in the kitchen, it was this presence that gave me the opportunity to get facts about the deceased woman in the flat. Amalie had worked as a party cook, and I knew I had to say this. True enough, there was a deceased cook named Amalie, who had lived in the flat several years earlier, and now she "was helping" the current tenant to keep tidiness in the kitchen and peace in the home as best she could. If Jette's family hadn't helped me here, I couldn't have been so precise. At the private level, I also often ask them for help to be able to support Jette in the best possible way.

THE DEAD BOY

Another very telling story is about one of my course participants. As a young man, his father was a football coach for a happy-go-lucky boy named Jesper. One day the boy and his father were on a trip to a flooded gravel pit when the boy suddenly experienced difficulties. His father tried to save him, but unfortunately, they both perished in the gravel pit. The tragedy made a big impression on my student's father, and several years later he baptised his own son Jesper to honour the boy and his family – despite there being a family tradition with other names in the family.

When my course participant Jesper was only a week old, he couldn't keep his breast milk down and vomited heavily after each breastfeeding. The new mother was worried and exhausted, but was turned away by the doctor, who shrugged it off by saying that infants can regurgitate a lot. However, Jesper's father insisted that something was wrong and contacted another doctor who immediately diagnosed a narrowing of the stomach which required surgery. His father's extra efforts saved Jesper's life. I sense that the father of the infant Jesper received support from the father and child who died in the gravel pit to save his boy. In that way, I also believe that the old story, where the father of the deceased Jesper couldn't save his son, was healed.

Many years later, Jesper was on an epigenetic healing course with me. In a deep healing meditation, where both his own father's and mother's relatives were present, it suddenly became clear that the deceased boy and his family were also supporting the healing processes. It happened because there was a very great gratitude towards Jesper's family for having honoured and valued the deceased boy and his lineage.

SUPPORT FROM OTHERS

Perhaps throughout this chapter you have been sitting thinking about what it is like if you are adopted. Here it is very important to know that there is support both from your biological lineage and from your adoptive family's lineage. You are actually doubly supported through a life that sometimes has more challenges than average. The same can apply to foster families or other important relationships that have been in your family.

Support lineages don't always have to be of human origin. I have on several occasions sensed elf-like lineages that support the healing. This can both be because there has been a deep contact between the spirit world and the ancestors in the lineage, and because there may be some karmic connections between my client and the spirit dimension in which elves and other such nature-beings move. In the next chapter I will write more about karmic healing.

YOU CAN DO IT YOURSELF

Like much else in this book, working epigenetically is definitely something you can practice with a healer, but you also have the opportunity to work with it yourself. Just like Sean from Hawaii has got me going back searching in my lineage, you can get started too. You can also look at your immediate family and see what patterns you are repeating from them. When you do a little exploring, you may find that treating each other badly or having a feeling of lacking something is repeated in several generations. If so, it could be a genealogical pattern. From there, you can go in and ask for help from your lineage to break the pattern so that it doesn't continue. First connect with the pillar of light, find peace in yourself, and then try to see if there is anyone in your lineage who may have struggled with the same themes you do. Try to open up to the fact that these relatives want to take responsibility, take back the pain and help heal both of you. Now try to feel where in your body a certain theme or pattern affects you, and ask that some relatives come forward who can help with it.

Look too at the positive traits that recur in your lineage. What talents are there, what contributions to the world, what are you proud of and happy about in your lineage? Where in your family can you see something that has succeeded and that you might also want to try yourself? Ask for help with that. Feel the energy of those who come. It doesn't have to be angels or something else exalted; it can simply be just the smell of Chloé perfume or the smoke from grandfather's cigar.

***

Sofie's story:
'MY GREAT-GREAT-GRANDFATHER'S APOLOGY CREATED A WAVE OF FORGIVENESS.'

When Sofie's father died recently, it was after a long life of drinking alcohol and forsaking Sofie. But the parting was beautiful and pure because, through contact with the spirit world, Sofie had managed to understand what was at stake in her lineage and thereby in her father. Her existential anxiety had disappeared.

"The deceased have always been in my life; I just didn't know what they were. In the house I grew up in as a child, there was a staircase by my room. Every evening I saw figures coming up the stairs, up towards me. I was scared out of my wits but didn't tell anyone.

I also acted out some role-plays that I could later see were probably repeats of previous lives. I just thought it was my imagination and that other people were also like that, but my friend thought it was deeply odd that I had this parallel fantasy world where I could involve people who weren't there in the game.

I have always dreamt a lot too. I have received several mysterious encounters with other beings in my dreams, which I always felt were just incredibly scary.

The fire is lit

Ten years ago, I went to a girls' night where there was a clairvoyant. I sat with both arms and legs crossed and thought it was so ridiculous; I wasn't open at all. The clairvoyant tuned in to each of us, saying, 'You have clairvoyance,' 'You have clear hearing,' and so on. When she came to me, she said, 'You have it all.' Then it was as if I caught fire. Today I know that it was the healing energy – that I simply woke up at that moment. It was shocking to go from being so sceptical to feeling that really deep down it was true, but it still scared me. I come from a family where that kind of thing isn't acceptable; in fact, it has been something that was mocked. The mere fact that I had trained as a psychotherapist was a bit too much – emotions and psychology were something strange, so also to come out and say that I could see people's souls, angels and nature-beings would cross so many boundaries. I therefore put the lid back on the box and joked that I was probably a witch.

Lost and lonely

The big change happens for me when I move to the countryside from Copenhagen. Out there I get several experiences; among other things I experience some deceased people standing staring at me out on my land. At the same time, I have a growing feeling of not being present in myself, not being happy, constantly feeling lost and lonely. One day I am driving in my car and, at a crossroads, I see a huge accident that isn't there. I can see the ambulance and some people lying on the road, and I'm sure something has happened there. It is so unpleasant and I know that I have to do something about it, so I write to Marzcia, saying that I would like to have a course entrance sitting. At the sitting, she says: 'You aren't just mature, you're overmature.' She describes it as a dam where the beavers have laid trees and says, 'When you lift them, it will flow completely freely within you.' So I start on a course with her but not with the aim that it should be with deceased contact, almost the opposite. After all, I haven't been experiencing the deceased as a resource but as something scary, an intrusion. But when I start doing clairvoyance sessions, they are simply swarming with deceased people. Now it is suddenly not scary at all anymore but incredibly touching and beautiful because they are coming with so much healing and restoration. For example, I have a woman for clairvoyance who is visited by her mother, who says she is sorry she gave her daughter the feeling of not being loved as much as her brother was. She had just found it difficult to express her love for her daughter because she had been jealous. It is so beautiful to see how the daughter feels the love from her mother who truly loved her but was unable to show it while she was alive. What I now discover about the deceased is that they are somewhat different from how they were in the life they lived.

They have entered into their soul essence and they come from a completely pure, loving place. They shift from being those who were plagued by the ego state, perhaps offensive, hurtful, dismissive or depressed, to the state their soul really is. From there, there is only warmth and the desire to want the best. I feel in the clairvoyance sessions that the deceased come in their purest form.

And so do my own deceased relatives.

A man with large hands

I meet my great-great-grandfather in an exercise on a course where we have to let those who come, come. The woman sitting with me is a little unsure of her deceased contact as she begins to describe an old environment. She says, 'I can hear horse-drawn carriages, cows and cobblestones. I see people in old clothes, but how are you going to recognise that?' I tell her she should try to stay in it as she describes a man who is an owner of an unknown establishment; he looks after it and runs it. 'There is a lot of activity and it is important that the work is done well,' she tells me in continuation. And then she says the man has large hands. Even before she says it, it is beginning to dawn on me because I know the history of my father's family, and now I'm quite sure. We have large hands in that line of the family, and I have inherited them. So now I am not in any doubt about who it is.

My great-great-grandfather was a tenant at a large place and had five sons. The youngest son was my great-grandfather. He fell in love with a very poor girl – my great-grandmother – and when he chose her, my great-great-grandfather disowned him because she wasn't good enough. The consequence was that my great-grandfather and great-grandmother came to live in deep poverty. They had lots of love and lots of children, but they were so poor that at one point they had made a living by selling seaweed for fuel.

Their lives had been full of hard work; they had to send my grandmother out as a servant as a five-year-old, where she would walk through town in the morning to light the fire at the house of the school principal. There was no room for feelings. It was hard work and toil from the start, because it was all a matter of survival. It became a life where you couldn't sit down and cry over things because there had to be food on the table. That way of living – or surviving – was passed on to my grandmother, who worked hard all her life. Almost as a parallel to my grandmother's early trips out as a servant to the gentry, as a child, my father had to go by himself to the kindergarten all the way through town. My grandparents had a restaurant, and when my father came home from school, he had to sit down and do his homework and then it was into the kitchen to help in the restaurant. In the evening, he would fall asleep under the tables and sleep there until they could close up and go home to bed. The next day it started all over again.

The responsibility lands in the right place

My father was highly sensitive, and I am fairly certain that my grandmother was too. But neither of them could allow themselves to make room for their sensitivity; they just had to work hard. So my father started drinking and he drank all my life. When I was eight, he had his first heart attack, and from then on, I was just waiting for him to die. I could always sense his vulnerability and knew that that was why he drank. In general, he was dreadful at looking after himself but, of course, that didn't change the fact that it was unpleasant. Just as my grandmother hadn't been able to take care of my father's sensitivity, even though she loved him deeply, neither could he take care of mine, and it has left traces in me that have made it difficult for me to accommodate my own and others' feelings.

My great-great-grandfather then comes in and takes responsibility for everything and apologises. Recognising that this wasn't the fault of my father, my grandmother or my great-grandfather is a huge relief. It started with my great-great-grandfather and now that he has accepted the responsibility, it has landed in exactly the right place.

Grandma's coldness turned to warmth

What happened that day primarily made me feel great compassion for my grandmother, whom I had always seen as a harsh lady – reprimanding, tight-lipped and critical. For example, I remember that she was furious at me once when, as a 15-year-old, I couldn't work out how to get a wash going. Today I can easily understand that it seems slovenly and lazy when I compare it to the conditions in which she grew up. I also understood why she couldn't take care of my father and his sensitivity. She thought the world of him, but she also had the part in her that said everyone must knuckle down. When my great-great-grandfather came forward and took his responsibility, I could suddenly understand his perspective. I could feel the wounded boy he had been, and I began to forgive.

The forgiveness helped me to let go of my anger and sadness at not being seen, and the coldness I experienced from my grandmother's side was turned to warmth and caring. The warmth was directed not just at my father, but also at me and the pattern I can occasionally have where I have a hard time accommodating my own and others' sensitivity. Even though I have been working on it for many years, I can say to my two children, for example, 'Now you have to pull yourselves together' when they are having a difficult time. But today I know that it comes from a desire for survival – a feeling that if we don't do this, we will perish. After that day, that feeling could be quietly put to rest.

Peace with my father

My father died two months ago. That for which I had been waiting since I was eight happened. The fear that my father would die and leave me, and I wouldn't be able to bear it, had been a huge part of my life. But it simply turned out so fine. He had become a shadow of himself in his final years. When I sat with him, he just listened and didn't say anything. He drank too much, ate too much and had diabetes. In the past, I had been plagued by grief and anger over his inability to just pull himself together and look after himself better. When he loved us so much, why couldn't he stop treating himself so badly? I knew very well that he really couldn't – he had also had a brain haemorrhage that had added to the problem – and yet I still had a fierce anger that he couldn't be adult and look after himself. After forgiving my great-great-grandfather, I let go of that fixation with my father and was able to see him more clearly and caringly, but not with pity in the way that I thought it was a shame for him. I had more of an acceptance that this was just how it was for him – and there is a trail back in time that explains why. The last six months, therefore, I was much more forgiving of him and could be at peace with him. There was a release – not from one day to the next, but in hindsight.

When I sat with him by his deathbed, it wasn't at all as I had been fearing: that there was still something I was missing, that he mustn't leave me. I was no longer a little girl who was lacking something, but an adult who had responsibilities. For me, it had been crucial to get in touch with the spirit world and know that we go back to something that will look after us because I knew he was just going to leave his body, but he would still be there for me. I healed and asked his guides to be with him. When he had finally taken his medicine and the last remnant of oxygen left him, I saw his soul leave his body and stand at the foot of the bed.

It said, 'It's okay, you've done what you were supposed to do – you're welcome to go.'

Then I left a couple of hours later. I just had to be ready because I knew very well that this had been the last time I had seen him alive. When they called in the morning and said he was dead, I drove back and fetched his things. They had opened the window at the hospital to let the soul fly out, but I had had contact with it and knew that it had already slipped away.

I drove from Jutland home to Copenhagen, and his soul sat next to me in the passenger seat all the way home and was as he was when he was at his best. I cried and laughed and was happy to feel that he was well – perhaps for the first time in years.

The anxiety is gone

Before, I had a feeling of sadness and a fear of living. I have always had a duality in me; on the one hand I throw myself into things and think, 'We have to do this,' and on the other hand I also think, 'Uh, uh, we'd better just stay put.' In this, the experience with my great-great-grandfather has liberated me. I can feel it all the way down to the micro level. For example, in the past, a situation like corona and worries about my economy would have had me in the foetal position. That's not the case anymore, because I know that it is a fear inherited from my lineage that everything will fall apart if I can't manage to get things tidied up, taken care of, and made proper. My life is not my father's, my grandmother's nor my great-grandfather's. I don't have to fight for my survival, and that realisation has come out of forgiveness. It is as if the line has been pulled back. My existential anxiety has disappeared."

***

Endnotes

7   Full original title: The Biology of Belief – Unleashing the Power of Consciousness, Matter & Miracles (2005). The anniversary edition from 2016 has some good updates compared to the one from 2005.

8   Remember that we don't incarnate our whole soul every time.

CHAPTER 6 – in brief

- Epigenetics means "besides the genes." It is the teaching about the genes we carry from our lineage. Genes can either be expressed or muted, and they dictate what potential we have.

- Your lineage holds both your options and your limitations Your deceased relatives will only wish the best for you because if you survive, the lineage survives. Even family members with whom you have had a hard time in life, now that they are freed from the weight of the life they lived, could be a great resource for you.

- There may be themes, beliefs and blockages in the lineage that you carry with you into your contemporary life. For example, it could be a theme like unhappy love or having problems getting the money to go around.

- Your lineage also has possibilities and positive qualities. Maybe there is one or more of them to whom you are similar in talents and interests and who you can enjoy meeting.

- When we are healed epigenetically, we often find out where the problem comes from and heal both the lineage and ourselves at the same time. In this way, we help our lineage both backwards and forwards in time, and ultimately it also means that we heal humanity as a whole.

**AT MARZCIA.DK YOU CAN
FIND THESE MEDITATIONS:**

Epigenetic lineage of mother and father

Mother's lineage

Father's lineage

KARMIC HEALING

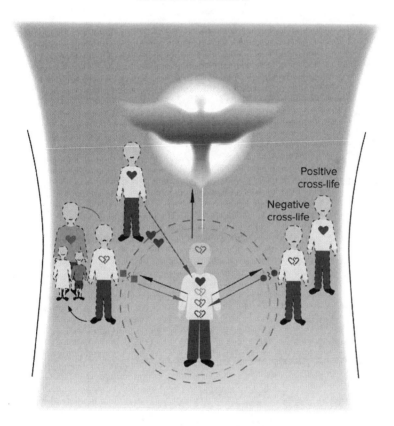

Positive
cross-life

Negative
cross-life

- ■ Karmic blockage from past life
- ● Epigenetic blockage from lineage
- ♥ Blockage is dissolved
- ♡ Blockage in the body
- ∿ Blockage in the soul

CHAPTER 7

KARMIC HEALING

About how your past lives can affect your present one

In the previous chapter, I wrote about how trauma or blockages in your lineage can affect you in your life today and how epigenetic healing can have major, positive consequences, not only for you in your current life, but also for your past lineage, your future lineage, and humanity. We are connected for so many generations, and we pass on what we are carrying – the good and the difficult – in our genes. Thus, when we heal the lineage, we ultimately heal all of us.

Karmically, we are also connected as human beings. Your soul is born many times; it may have lived in many incarnations before, and everything it has experienced is part of your current life in some form or another. On the one hand, this means that there may be themes and challenges from past lives that still affect your life today and that you therefore need your soul's past experiences healed. On the other hand, your soul also carries positive experiences and wisdom, which you can access with great benefit if you come into contact with your past lives. Karmic work is thus much more than good stories; there is a lot of learning, releasing, healing and development to be found in it. Like epigenetic healing, karmic healing also affects humanity and our history on and with the Earth – and not just the history of us humans; I often find that clients or course participants come into contact with previous lives where they weren't human and which don't even have a physical form. Karmic healing thus has the potential to heal all living consciousness in the universe, regardless of dimension.

THE BODY KNOWS THE TRAUMA
One of the theorists I am inspired by when it comes to karmic work is the American psychologist Michael Newton (1931–2016). He worked with regression therapy, a well-known concept in psychology, which is about leading clients back to earlier times in their life and dealing with the problem where it has arisen. Michael Newton went a step further and worked with leading clients back to previous lives. His basic idea was that the themes, experiences, and challenges we have had in past lives can have an impact on our present lives. In other words, we pass on our trauma from life to life. According to Newton, it is connected like this: when you were born, your soul came down into your body with the intent of collaborating with your physical form and with the beliefs already implanted in it. I am convinced we face both past lives and epigenetic challenges when the soul needs to collaborate with the body and again, of course, all the good things. The feelings, blockages and traumas that your soul has experienced before were thus already present in the body you were born into. You therefore weren't born as a whole new and fresh body, free from blockages as you might think, but in a body that matched what your soul had experienced before. It may well be that your soul had "forgotten" the limitations or blockages that existed in a previous life; it might have just been eagerly looking forward to coming down and living and experiencing again, but the moment it was incarnated, that is, came down into a heavier frequency, the limitations also came back. Admittedly, the soul always takes its experiences with it to the other side – having lived a life on Earth is significant for soul growth. But sometimes we don't finish what we are doing on Earth; there are themes that we don't deal with properly while we are here and then it may be that we come back to get them healed. The trauma still hangs there, but it really belongs to a past life and can therefore be difficult to understand in this

life. For example, if you were burned at the stake as a witch in a previous life, you may feel that you aren't allowed to speak out loud about your spirituality today. You don't know where the belief comes from. It is just strong within you; you are afraid to speak out because it is sitting deep inside you that it is dangerous. It could also be that you are afraid to express your views altogether, not because something in this life dictates that you need to be afraid of it, but perhaps because you have been beaten by your husband or ostracised from society in a past life. The beliefs don't really correspond to the happy, free soul you are, but at the moment you were incarnated and came down into a physical form you also came into contact with the challenges that have been in your previous physical lives, again. And that is when we have problems.

I often have course participants who have worked really hard on themselves in this life, yet they constantly face the same challenges and just can't get past them. They have come a long way in working with their current lives; they may have gone to a psychologist or other therapists, and they have done a really good job. But for some reason that is hidden from themselves, they can't really get hold of the last part of the solution and move on. Perhaps you are also familiar with that feeling – as if you are constantly falling into the same emotional trap or feel like you are knocking on the same door without being able to open it, even though you really want to. It is as if something is missing. The knot simply feels insoluble, and for good reasons. A karmic trauma is often much more locked-in than other traumas. I experience this clearly when I sit in front of a person with karmic problems. I can quite simply feel that the stuff with which they struggle is as old and hard as the clearest black lava stone. I get a deep feeling that I am being led past this life and into something else that is lying there like an intense, locked area. But even if it feels insoluble, it isn't hopeless; on the contrary, because when we know that everything we have experienced in previous lives lies in our consciousness and that the soul, body, thoughts and feelings work together, we can start working with our traumas, based on ordinary trauma therapy.

YOUR INNER HITCHHIKER

Karmic healing can be extremely liberating if you are ready for it. It can take a long time to become ready to deal with a trauma, but the trauma remains there until we take care of it. We could try to get away from it, but it is a bit like driving past a roadside hitchhiker and continuing to pass him until we finally pick him up and discover that he is actually a part of ourselves that we have been trying to avoid. My explanation is that when our souls need to incarnate again, we physically, mentally and emotionally contact the places we have previously been with our souls, where there has been some unprocessed stuff that we are here to process this time around. There is nothing wrong with that, but there is something we have deposited on our way – left like a hitchhiker who was never picked up. When we are born again, we will have to take care of it because this time we are better equipped to handle the task, and the karmic work becomes really interesting at this point. Our karmic incarnations can thus help us to understand our current traumas or beliefs just as we can heal on old issues and liberate that part of our soul essences that we haven't been able to grasp without going into past lives.

Michael Newton's theory was that the greater the trauma we have experienced on Earth, the sooner we come back. Maybe you remember the Swedish woman Barbro Karlén, whom I mentioned in Chapter 2. She was born in 1953, only nine years after Anne Frank, her previous incarnation, had died. Anne Frank had lived precisely that, a life containing a lot of violence, and suffered a terrible, traumatic death. The American child psychiatrists Ian Stephenson and Jim Tucker have similarly worked with children, who talk about memories from their previous lives. These are children who can have no knowledge of the people, places and events they are talking about. In this work too, it is clear that those who have suffered a very violent death can quickly come back again with the horrors in their baggage. It is as if they haven't managed to digest the impressions completely. Either the shock has been so violent that it is still being activated into memory when they return and are about to be born. Or the karmic traumas may have a physical expression: children whose incarnation has been shot in a previous life may have marks on the body similar to the place where the bullet hole had been. Fortunately, it is rare to see it expressed so graphically, and that isn't at all what I mostly see in my practice. Nor is it always the case that my clients or students have an awareness of having lived before, such as Barbro Karlén and the children in Stephenson's and Tucker's studies. But I see a lot of examples of past beliefs, blockages or unresolved traumas causing problems in this life. We can, however, do something about that.

FROM HOUSE CLEANSING TO KARMIC HEALING

When I work with karmic healing, I connect the experience I have as a medium and healer with the work of Michael Newton, Ian Stephenson and Jim Tucker – as well as with the trauma theory I have learnt through my SE training. Based on these different theories, I work using my experience and the understanding I have of the soul and its desire to move forward. It provides a fusion of methods that I see gives some powerful processes for release.

One of the experiences on which I frequently draw is the one I have gathered through house cleansing. The very essence of house cleansing or liberation of souls for me is to see that we are dealing with a soul that for some reason remained hanging onto a physical plane instead of going over into the pillar of light. The soul has been repressed by the patterns of the living person. I usually call it an unresolved deceased. The deceased person thinks that home is the physical home, not the spiritual one, most often because the deceased person, who is told that it is his turn to die, thinks, "I belong here. I have built this house for myself, my wife and my children. My son was born here – I'm staying here." Thus, for this deceased person, "home" is the earth-bound house and not between lives or in the soul home. It really makes good sense, I think, that it is confusing and transgressive for this deceased person when new people come along and live in "its" house. In house cleansing, I have often come out to a deceased person who is very angry about something or other. He may be angry that living in his house now is a young man, who has started tearing down the kitchen walls and building a bathroom instead. It can also be that the deceased person has lived in a time when women didn't have as much to say as they do today, and now the deceased has difficulty dealing with the fact that a woman owns, and makes the decisions in, his home. I quite often come up against old male authorities who have a very hard time with a single woman running his house. This creates problems for the living woman. For example, I once did a house cleansing for a Saturday night TV show. I visited an independent woman who owned a farm with three outbuildings. She had a strong sense that someone was watching her and she was feeling really uncomfortable about it. At this place, I found out that there was a deceased person who had owned the farm and was really angry that she wanted to tear some of the outbuildings down, because the farm had been his life's work. He had been under pressure because he had had a big responsibility to take care of his family farm. Now along came this woman, who wasn't related to him and who had some ideas which for him were very far-out. I entered into a dialogue with him and said, "Listen, it's a different time now. For you, it's time to go." Through the healing and support that came to him from the spirit world and his lineage, he began to relax and could finally let go and meet his family on the other side. They welcomed him and were happy that he had come home and could be free of his physical life. In this case, the healing meant that the deceased man let go of the over-responsibility he had manifested in anger. There could finally be peace on the farm.

Experiences like these help when I am working with karmic healing today. In fact, parts of the living person's soul essence have often been held, mentally or emotionally, in unfulfilled beliefs and therefore haven't gone into the pillar of light when death occurred. When that trauma is dissolved not only the deceased person but the living one is greatly liberated when the person gains access to the potential of his soul essence, which has been lying in an unresolved deceased incarnation.

THE BOY WHO COULDN'T SAVE HIS SISTER

Let me give an example of this. Imagine that in a previous life you were a little boy in the 18th century. Your family was poor, there was famine, and your parents had died. They had left you with a little sister who they said you had to take care of. You were of course too little for such a responsibility, and you couldn't live up to it either, so you both died of starvation. Your grief and your bad conscience over having let her down meant that your soul didn't go completely into the light. Part of your soul essence remained trapped in the old trauma along with the experience of famine, panic and pain.

Now, in this life, you may be affected by the feeling of being insufficient, of taking on too much responsibility and still not being able to live up to it, and perhaps you are also affected by the fear that there won't be enough food because you have experienced famine. Even though you are living a completely different life now, you still have many of the same beliefs and are beginning to relive some of the same traumas as the little orphaned boy. Even though a belief originates from a completely different time and a completely different life, there may be some themes in your life that are reminiscent of it – for example, the fear of not having enough, that you may not be able to take care of those closest to you or that you are insufficient. Your nervous system is simply responding to something that doesn't correspond to the reality in which you are living now – you can take good care of your loved ones and there is no need to fear famine.[9]

I can now get in touch with the little boy you were in a previous life. Through this contact I get his story and understand why he is so sad and what has prevented him from going completely over into the light. Maybe it turns out he had to take care of his sister and he couldn't. He really tried, but she died of starvation. Perhaps I see that the boy has been preoccupied with the fact that he lost his sister, that he was insufficient and couldn't keep his promise. Even though his mother, father and his little sister were all waiting for him in the pillar of light when he died, he was so sad that he couldn't even see the light. He was simply locked in his depressed feelings. It is clear part of his soul has, of course, gone into the light because otherwise his experiences wouldn't have manifested in you today. However, his traumatic experiences and his self-perception is still blocked. I therefore let the healing contact him and quietly pray that everyone from the spirit world who can help will come forward. As a healer, I am only the channel, so I can't help him. But when I ask for help, the whole family rushes forward. They shout eagerly; they so want to help him, and he is greeted in that presence. He raises his gaze a little and begins to feel the warmth and love. His trauma loosens and he begins to have confidence that all is well. As soon as he releases the heavy vibrations, he can go into the light. He feels that he is loved unconditionally even though he couldn't save his sister. The sister is just happy with how much effort he really made to take care of her back then, and she is fine now – he can see that because she is smiling and whole and safe. His father says to him: "What a good job you made of that. I am sorry I died prematurely and left you with the responsibility. It was too much for you." His mother just loves him deeply. Suddenly, all his potential to feel loved and good enough comes to the fore, and then his blockages disappear. Now the contours of his physical form disappear; at least that is what often happens for me. So now his physical form has been completely dissolved into the soul essence. The boy becomes a lighter consciousness, full of joy, feelings of being sufficient, success and love. That is the capacity in your soul essence that you, who are still lying on my massage table as a client, have been lacking in this life. But now that the trauma is resolved. You can integrate that part of your soul essence that feels you are worthy, loved and sufficient. Before, you had your focus on everything that made you feel you could do nothing right, but with the help of karmic healing, you have now said goodbye to that belief and can go out into the world in a completely different way. You can simply see all the places where you are succeeding. All mental, physical and emotional blockages are healed and liberated, as a shining consciousness, which in reality is the soul essence belonging to your potential, arises. That potential is integrated into you during the healing, and you are presented with many more possibilities in your current life.

THE GIRLFRIEND RELATIONSHIP IS HEALED

Karmic work can also loosen up relationships. The little boy who couldn't save his sister was in a complicated relationship with his sister, his mother and his father. From my point of view, we most often come down into some of the same soul constellations, so you may well experience that in this life you have difficulties with some living people, either because you two are meeting again in a new life and now have the opportunity to do healing on something from the past or because the theme itself is karmic and you need to do healing on it to move on with being able to be in healthy relationships. Maybe you have separation anxiety in relation to your girlfriend because the little boy you once were hasn't been able to process what went badly back then. When you are healed karmically, you can also relax and feel that you are sufficient in your couple relationship. That way, it isn't only you and your soul that are being healed, but also the relationships you have. It spreads like ripples in the water. You are healed, your relationship is healed, and the person with whom you are in a relationship will also have the opportunity for growth. If you have a trauma connected into the relationship, it is as if you are holding each other fixed with heavy, black chains. If you release the trauma, the chains become super elastic bands that connect you and at the same time allow for expansion, space and the trust that things can go well and that you don't have to let go of each other. There will be more room for manoeuvre on a better foundation in the relationship.

YOU HAVE GOLD WITH YOU TOO IN YOUR BAGGAGE

Even though there can be so many bad and difficult events from our previous lives, there is also an enormous positive potential in lives where things have gone well for the incarnation. The difference between the good lives and the lives where there has been trauma or negative belief is that where the "bad" lives need healing and liberation in order for the soul essence to be liberated between the lives, then the soul essence from the "good" life is completely free and over in the pillar of light between the lives; here there are no incarnations to be healed. However, you can still have the opportunity to experience those lives – like a form of a knowledge bank or soul memory – and enrich yourself by both healing and insight. We can experience great joy from encountering and becoming aware of abilities and experiences from here.

At one point, I found out for myself that I had been a spiritual teacher in a previous life. I saw a woman teaching a group of people healing and contact with the divine out in a forest, perhaps in the Middle Ages. Because I got in contact with her, I also got in contact with her experience and wisdom. Through her, I gained access to qualities that were in my soul but to which I hadn't had access before. I discovered that, over several centuries, I had built up a capacity to do what I do today and it gave me both an extra trust in my own abilities and a calmness to settle into my work. I believe that everyone can gain insight into their qualities through past lives. If we work karmically, we can find space and access to the good lives. I don't think it is a coincidence that you are good at precisely what you are good at – whether it is something creative, something spiritual or perhaps a special flair for money and business. I believe that what we are really good at is something we have honed through many lives and often have also fought and worked hard for. Just as we stand on the shoulders of our ancestors, we also stand on the shoulders of our souls' past life experiences so that we can do what we can do today. Your talents aren't just those you have been given out of the blue; you have worked hard for them and therefore you can also confidently trust them. You have a deep foundation.

DO IT YOURSELF – IF YOU ARE READY

Karmic healing has enormous potential – we can use the karmic work constructively in our current lives to both do healing on traumas from past lives and to gain access to good qualities in ourselves. But karmic work can also be intense, both because it can be about violent traumas and because the actual resolution of the old traumas can be difficult. On many occasions, clients with whom I work experience the shocks, the traumas and the fears that the previous incarnation has been through. I have seen students and clients who were almost suffocating because their previous incarnations had involved drowning or they suddenly got the feeling that they had no leg because that leg had been chopped off in a previous life. You can therefore access a violent event, but here it is important to be able to say, "What is happening right now isn't you today. It is a part of you that is healing."

Since the karmic work can be intense, it is extra important to be prepared. As a healer, I always ask myself if I can sense that something is karmic, whether it is okay to take it now or whether the client or student would rather wait until she is more ready for it. Karmic healings can often take a long time too – there are so many layers that need to fall into place and integrate into current life that it can take months to work through. Along the way, the client can experience both mental and physical symptoms because she comes into contact with themes that are ancient.

Sometimes the spirit world itself shows signs that the time has come for a person to work karmically. Perhaps you start dreaming about past incarnations, reading about reincarnation or pondering the subject without knowing why. It is as if both the spirit world and your own system are trying to give some small sign that you should go that way.

It is quite possible to work karmically on your own. I started working with karmic healing without having much experience with it, and yet it happened.

I was in my mid-twenties and had taken Reiki 1. One day I went to a healer and clairvoyant, who nowadays is one of my close colleagues. She did a regression course with me and suddenly it was as if a barn door opened and lots of past lives passed by like pictures. I had no method or way of going about it, and actually I also had a great deal of resistance to my spiritual abilities at the time, so I didn't feel like relating to it. It so happened that for a while I had been living in my parents' backyard. I had no money and, on top of that, I had a sore throat – I was wretched. One of my acquaintances from the riding club had taken an application form for a clairvoyance training for me a few months earlier, but I had just put it to one side. Now that I was sick and completely miserable, I fell asleep and dreamt that I was a nun who had become pregnant with a troubadour. He had left me; the child had been taken from me and, in my unhappy state of mind, I had hung myself. When I woke up from that dream, I couldn't speak at all; my throat was completely constricted. But I sat down and filled out the application form for the training. For me, that story is about the fact that I had to relate to this earlier incarnation as a nun to take a small step further in acknowledging my spiritual abilities. I also found out, by working further with this incarnation, that some of my distrust of both people and the divine stemmed from this, just as my eternal throat problems did. It was old stuff and, although it was part of my soul's past experiences, it didn't need to manifest itself in this life.

My feeling is quite clear that if you start to get in touch with your soul essence and gain access to past lives, then you may as well start working on it yourself. The important thing, however, is that you are able to stay in your soul essence and your current life so that you are not overwhelmed by the themes of your past life. The themes of past lives are deeply encoded in your consciousness and your feelings, even all the way into your bones, so you need to be really well centred in yourself so as not to get caught in or overwhelmed by them. If you encounter a previous incarnation, you must be able to identify, "This is certainly a good incarnation or this is an incarnation that needs healing and help to get into the dimension of the pillar of light."

CONNECT WITH YOUR GUIDES

As with all other healing work, it is important that you are at peace, connected to the pillar of light and with karmic healing; it is also important that you are well-connected with your guides so that you have as much backup as possible. A lot of healing energy has to be used for karmic processes. If you get into working with your own healing potential and, for example, you experience an incarnation as a little boy who needs help to release something traumatic, you can ask both those who can help him to come forward and that healing from the spirit world can flow through with love. Then you will find that there is someone who will take care of it. Your task is only to support and show the way. There are some others who take over. If you follow the guidelines, you will be able to do a lot yourself. However, if you have major karmic themes, having a professional such as a karmic healer or a regression therapist, to help you can be crucial. I think that if you do regressions without the healing perspective, the client may go through some rather heavy experiences and leave with the feeling that there is nothing to it or that it will just become an interesting or dramatic story. And that is why I call my method karmic healing and not regression. There is so much meaning to get out of working with past lives not just for the individual but indirectly for many more people and on multiple planes.

***

Signe's story:
'I COULD ONLY SEE THE BAD THINGS IN OUR RELATIONSHIP BEFORE'

Nine years ago, Signe, who is now 34, was so depressed that she just wanted to disappear from this life. Instead of the anti-depressant medication she was being offered, she chose healing, and it not only gave her the desire to be here on Earth, but also paved the way for a wonderful family life with the boyfriend she had in fact left.

"When I was 25, I had a period where I was very sad. I was on a tough, competitive course of studies along with several hundred other students where you were just a number in the row. I generally had a feeling of not being able to reach out to humans or animals. There were many mornings where I lay in bed discussing with myself whether I should get up and go to school or just disappear. If you didn't turn up, you couldn't go to the exam or get your student grant. The only thing that was getting me in there was the thought that I would lose my grant money.

In the end, I went to the doctor and after a long conversation was offered antidepressant medication. I was advised to go home and think about it and then come back. In between the two visits to the doctor, my brother, who is nine years older than me and had made contact with the spiritual world early on, said that I should go and see Marzcia, whom he knew well. She had a one-day healing course where you could test your abilities. I went to it, and it felt absolutely wild. I reacted very intensely to it; I felt ill and dizzy and, although I was normally a very shy and inhibited person back then, I couldn't stop the words pouring out of me in front of the others, gabbling such things as 'I can't make head nor tail of this!' When we were going to stop, several healers had to get me grounded again before I could walk. It all touched me deeply and I could feel that I was in the right place. In fact, I wasn't any worse than I had been before; now I could just feel it and it was a little overwhelming.

I refused the antidepressants and started instead on Reiki 1 with Marzcia, after which I continued on Angels 1 and all sorts of other courses. In the time following, I didn't get any better – more the contrary. I became increasingly aware of how sensitive I really am. It was good to find out because then I could do something about it, but it was also really tough.

At the first module on karmic healing, we had an exercise where we had to fetch resources from a previous, good life into this life. When doing this, I saw a previous life where I was a male elf living out in the woods, very content with his life. He went around gathering herbs, and I saw that there were crystals and healing of the plants' energy. I took in his deep contact with nature and through that I got a lot of contact with elves and the way they live with nature. This got me through my studies. I got a deep connection with the hardcore biochemistry I was supposed to know there, and when I was reading, I got the feeling of being surrounded by an elf soul family. Even though that course was just about the place I had felt most alone, I now got a feeling of not being alone any more.

A problematic relationship

At the time, I had an ex-boyfriend, Kasper, who I talked to every day. We had been a couple and had separated, but we could figure out neither how to let go of each other nor become a real couple again. Our relationship had been marked by a lot of quarrels and pain. I was full of projections and blamed Kasper for how I felt. My low self-esteem became, 'You aren't good enough to make me feel good.' Sometimes I was also so frustrated and upset inside that it would feel good to move the pain outside of myself by starting a quarrel because then it wasn't me that was the pain, it was 'the world.' We would also argue a lot about money, which for me was associated with something very hard, without me knowing why. I felt insecure in the world and projected it onto him.

We had therefore stopped being a couple and had moved away from each other, but we still couldn't let go.

In the last module of karmic healing, we had to look into a future life, where we had solved a problem in our current life, and thereby perhaps be able to solve it better or quicker in this life. The day we were going to do this, I was really sad. It can be pretty tough to be going through karmic healing, and I was in a really bad mood and quite resigned about it all. I didn't know what to ask for, so I asked the spirit world and got the answer: 'Ask to see what love looks like when love works.' I wasn't thinking in terms of relationships at all but thought that I should see love in an angelic life, that I would go to the elves or something else wonderful – not something on Earth that I really resisted. Yet it so happened that I saw a kitchen-dining room, which was furnished with a large table, where bowls were going around, and four or five children of different ages were sitting around the table enjoying themselves. There was also a very handsome man of whom I could only see the chest, but I had the sense of a huge, radiant heart. I was really fascinated by him, but I was also resisting because he was a human being. Marzcia kept saying I should go there, but I was really struggling with that. At one point she said, 'Does it make sense that you have some resistance to coming back as a human being?' She was right, so I had to work on that first.

Cherish the love

A year later, Kasper and I got together again. I had been in a trainee job in another town, and Kasper had come along as a friend to get a break from his life in Copenhagen, and it turned out to be really good for us to get away from our everyday lives, which we found a little stressful, and just be together somewhere close to nature. When we returned to Copenhagen and were about to move into separate apartments, we decided instead to move in together and try to become a couple again. We took it gently and this time it went much better. I had gained respect for the fact that there isn't just a boyfriend and then another boyfriend – you have to take care of the love you get. So I cherished our relationship better, not driving so many of my own projections into it. I could only see the bad things in our relationship before and could put all the problems into words, but never the good things. It was my own inability to dare to believe in love – that I could be loved and that I could love someone else, that it could be good.

A little while into our relationship, I recalled the meditation on a future life again, and since then I have been back to it several times because it turned out that there were a lot of things that were solved in it. First and foremost was my resistance to being human, which Marzcia had felt. Then my almost claustrophobic resistance to children and family. I had never really seen that being in a family could be a good thing. Or rather, I had shut off to the idea. I thought it would always be difficult to be close to someone, just as it was difficult for Kasper and me to be close to each other, and when children came, it would get even worse. But in the meditation, I saw myself as a strong woman who was good at being a mother to those children, with a feeling that I really had something good to give them. That woman had simply solved many of the problems with which I had struggled so much. There was also prosperity in the meditation – there had to be some money for that kitchen-dining room! I had believed that money was really hard to earn.

A lot of those problems were karmic. I have been into my previous lives and had to free myself from being crushed by an excessively difficult working life.

The spiritual plane manifests itself

Since Kasper and I became a couple again, it has been really good between us. We got married, had a baby and have moved away from the city again. Having that distance and living completely on our own is good for us. We have become really good at talking about everything. We both grew up keeping our feelings to ourselves a little bit, and it is just really uncomfortable, but we are never passive-aggressive any more. It has been difficult because we have forced ourselves to look at what each of us have in our baggage, but it is also really good, much better than I had dared to imagine.

I don't think I could have the life I have today if I hadn't developed through my spiritual side, which has been the fertile soil for the physically-lived life becoming as good as it has become and for me being able to feel so well and thrive in my surroundings. It was necessary to start there to find peace in myself. I have had to go in and deal with my basic beliefs about life being tough and there not being any point in being sensitive because then you will be trampled.

My feeling is that every time I have taken a big step forward with my spiritual side, it has later manifested itself in the physical world. And I can't do it the other way around; I can't first find the right job and then be okay with it inside or find the right relationship and then be okay with that inside. It sounds banal, but it is actually very powerful.

I think that if I hadn't talked to my brother at the time, I would have taken the antidepressants I had been offered, and it would probably have turned into more medication down the line. But it wouldn't have helped because the problem wasn't that I had an imbalance in the brain, but that I wasn't living in accordance with my soul and had too many knots to be able to feel that there was anything good. Kasper and I might well have found each other again, but it would have been very difficult with medication and maybe on social security because I don't think I would have got through my education without them.

A wonderful life

The biggest and hardest nut to crack was probably choosing to be here at all. I didn't want to be here, I felt enormously alone and sad. I couldn't reach out, but I couldn't handle life alone either. It was like one big knot that was only resolved when I began listening inwardly to my soul and a wisdom that knew more than what the 25-year-old me knew at the time. During the years when I was having a very hard time, it was as if I couldn't find a place in myself that had security, connectedness and joy, and therefore I couldn't point to it in my past either. Had I actually had a pleasant childhood? I couldn't feel it. But the more that the light, soul energy and fullness has come into my life, the more I can remember how very much love there was, especially from my Mum and Dad. It was a layer I hadn't been open to at all before, and it did a lot to heal my life today – it gave me so much light along the way.

My life is so wonderful now. It can of course be difficult at times, but in a completely different way. I don't think I was ever seriously at risk of committing suicide, but I have often thought that if I had been able to do away with myself without all sorts of death scenarios, I would have done so.

I am in a completely different place now; I can endure my son's crying or Kasper and I arguing. It doesn't cause everything to fall apart any more. There is more light than darkness now – it tipped for me in those years, from darkness, pain and evil filling most, to today where there are just small clumps of darkness. Now I can also see myself going through life and maybe even growing old.

I never thought I was going to make it to thirty. But now I am even looking forward to my next lives."

***

Ida Sofie's story:
'I WAS SCARED BEFORE; NOW I HAVE PEACE'

For many years, 17-year-old Ida Sofie was plagued by doors slamming and objects moving themselves,

especially in her room in the house her grandmother once owned. A house cleansing surprisingly showed that she has very special support from the spirit world. It has provided peace and surplus energy for the sensitive girl who has never felt completely at home in her own time.

"For as long as I can remember I have heard the sounds of doors slamming and seen objects moving. I haven't seen the dead, but I have dreamt a lot about them. For example, I once dreamt of my grandfather standing by a wood-burning stove. The next day, my dog stood looking at where my grandfather had been in my dream. These happenings have always been there, but there was a period when it kind of escalated. I didn't dare sleep in my room in my grandmother's house for a whole year because I was having such a hard time. If there was a cupboard that opened or a book that moved, I couldn't find peace in myself at all because I didn't know what was happening. I also had a lot of headaches and tried meditation and physiotherapy, but nothing helped.

When Marzcia and her team came out for a house cleansing at our place, they discovered that we had more than twelve spirits scattered throughout the house. Upstairs in my room, there was one called Peder. He was my great-great-great-grandfather; he had a daughter who had been taken away from him and he had been subjected to blows to his head.

The team asked if they should remove him. When they said that, I got an empty, sad feeling inside. I felt sad at what had been done to him; I could feel that it was inside me as something I had experienced myself. It suddenly made sense even in relation to the anxiety I had felt in my room. The team did a lot of healing on him, but I didn't want to have him removed. I knew he only wanted the best for me. So he was allowed to stay along with some of the other deceased who were related to us, my mother's grandmother and grandfather, for example. The rest were removed.

Now I had peace. It was like when you have a ringing in your ears and then it stops. I could suddenly think clearly again and had the energy to solve some other problems.

Out of place in the world

I have always felt different from others. I very often feel that I am out of place in the world in which I live. It may sound a little crazy, but it is like the world is a little too modern for me. I look back in time a lot and imagine how it was. I think history is exciting. I also like to be outside, picking berries and being with animals, and I have occasionally dreamt of myself in old clothes – as if I am in the wrong time. I just think that it seemed really nice in the old days. The house cleansing has given me peace with all that; it was a kind of explanation for me feeling that way. It has also become easier for me to have a sense of myself. Before, in school, I took in everything that the others felt. I didn't really have the time and space to get a sense of myself. Now I have time for something else. I will definitely use my spiritual side in the future. I would like to take some courses and meet other young people to whom I can talk about spirituality without feeling weird. My closest friend doesn't really believe in that kind of thing, so she is a little hard to talk to about it. I have started in a new class which is a little more spiritual. They work with crystals, and it's very nice that I don't have to feel strange any more. I haven't shared this particular experience with them because I still feel a little different and vulnerable.

The dead move too

We have just moved from my paternal grandmother and grandfather's house, and I was sad to be moving, especially from the garden, where I always felt happy and spent an awful lot of my time. When we moved, I said to the dead beings: 'You just come along.' I didn't feel that they belonged to the house; my mother's grandmother hasn't even been in the house. She just has a connection to my mother. And Peder hasn't been in the house either; he has a connection to me. So I thought that if we moved on, they would like to move with us. They had connections to us, not to the house.

I occasionally use the deceased by imagining that I am holding them by the hand and as I stand in a light. Then I gain some strength and confidence. Peder in particular is someone from whom I can always seek help. He is like a grandfather to whom I can just run and give a big hug. I think being discovered was good for Peder too. Just as he understands me, I understand him. And my Mum and I will try to find out more about him when it is possible. I was scared before; now I have peace."

***

<h2 style="text-align:center">Charlotte's story:
'WE REALLY NEEDED HELP'</h2>

Ida Sofie's mother, Charlotte, is happy and relieved that Ida Sofie has found peace and confidence in the meeting with her great-great-great-grandfather. And the rest of the family has let go of the feeling of being extras in their own lives.

"Ida Sofie has always had open channels, ever since she was very young. For example, she would say, 'Tomorrow we're going to get a new car,' and then her grandmother on her Dad's side would call the next day and say, 'Would you like to have our car?' Over time, we have had house cleansings and, in general, support from Marzcia, who I met at a lecture six or seven years ago and with whom have since taken various courses. However, at one point I fell ill and didn't have contact with her for a long time. Suddenly one day she sent a message out about a free house cleansing, and then the whole team came home to us.

Everything was going wrong

At that time, we really needed help in our family. We had a sense of being extras in our own lives. Things were going wrong all the time and we didn't understand why. For example, both toilets got blocked on the precise day we were having twenty children for a children's birthday party. There were also slamming doors and shadows in the hallway. It simply felt as if there was no room for us in the house in which we lived. Ida Sofie was anxious, and my son, who is a year and a half younger than her, had seen dead people. He could come and say, 'I met an old lady last night.' The house was bewitched.

At the same time, Ida Sofie had some difficult years. She has always been different. She is sensitive, presentient and can feel what everyone is feeling: who is angry and who is upset. In our view, this is a positive, but it has also been very lonely for her. And then she has had some interests that were completely different from those of other girls in her class, who were preoccupied with clothes and make-up. Ida Sofie was busy with old activities like crocheting, pickling and picking berries.

Peder's love

When Marzcia and the team came out to cleanse the house, we found out that Ida Sofie's great-great-great-grandfather Peder was in her room. During his life, there had been a violent incident in which he was surrounded and beaten and had his daughter from a previous marriage taken from him. We don't know much about it, but it was a really ugly incident. Suddenly Ida Sofie's anxiety and headaches made sense. But Peder only wished the best for her. He had thrown his love on Ida Sofie because she reminded him a lot of his daughter. I am actually convinced that she is his daughter. For example, she is completely magical in relation to sheep and lambs, and Peder was a sheep breeder. We also know that Ida Sofie physically resembles his daughter. So I think that Peder and Ida Sofie have a special connection in that he has felt misunderstood by those around him, just as Ida Sofie has.

More joy and peace
In the past, Ida Sofie was introverted and quiet because she felt so different. Now she has become more joyful and a little more outgoing. I don't know if it was about her self-esteem, insecurity or inner joy, but something at least has happened in that regard. For us as a family, the house cleansing brought peace to everything. They found an incredible amount during that cleansing: both dear relatives who were allowed to stay and angry deceased, like the one, for example, who went around slamming the doors in the basement because he was angry that we had done things in the house that he didn't like. The spirits that didn't belong to us were cleansed out.

The whole experience was fantastic; there was enormous joy and relief after some really difficult years. I had been having a hard time for such a long time. Even though I went to Marzcia, I was closed, feeling bad, having nausea and experiencing headaches. For many people, a house cleansing might be too powerful, but I really advise others to try and discreetly find some information. It gives me tremendous joy to know that my grandmother and grandfather are with me. A happiness and a trust."

***

WHEN YOUR SOUL CROSSES ITS TRACKS

Now we have looked at both epigenetic and karmic healing. In fact, there is sometimes a congruity between the two in the way that your incarnation in a previous life is also your own deceased relative. The traumas or the good qualities you have from that incarnation are therefore also inherited in your lineage. This is known as the cross-life. Remember that there is a difference between your DNA, the genetic imprint of your lineage and the "DNA" of your soul, which is divine essence, mental consciousness and emotional consciousness earned through the soul's journey through several lives. There is often a good opportunity to gain access to an important soul essence in the cross-life – whether it is trauma stuff that keeps the soul essence in abeyance or the good qualities and talents from the "good" lives in the lineage that strengthen you. In these cases, the healing will take place as an interplay between the lineage, which comes to heal and support, and the karmic healing, where an incarnation must be healed so that the client can either integrate the missing part of the soul essence or get in touch with several of the good qualities from the "good" incarnations. These cross-lives are often very important for the life you have today. They often help to unfold your life purpose and are part of the soul's reason for being in this life.

Endnote

9   We might ask why we generally suffer from supply anxiety when we have been living in an affluent society for generations now – just think of how we reacted when coronavirus first shut down the country and we all started hoarding from the supermarkets. According to logic, we shouldn't have a need for full shelves in our homes because we can just go shopping. But there are really a lot of us who have the need anyway. I myself am afraid

of running out of food, even though I haven't experienced it in this life. My fridge is always bulging even though it also means that I am going to produce food waste, which is directly against my inner biologist's values.

CHAPTER 7 – in brief

- The soul is immortal and doesn't have trauma and negative beliefs, but there can be unresolved states with which the soul comes into contact when it and physical life "meet" each other in a new incarnation.
- There are countless examples of children being able to talk about the people they have been in previous lives.
- Sometimes your soul has to be incarnated many times to resolve a trauma. It is a bit like a hitchhiker that you pass by time and again until you pick him up and discover that he is an aspect of yourself.
- There are plenty of good lives where you can use the contact to past lives to support yourself in strengthening your talents, qualities or other areas in which you would like help. These lives constitute openings for your qualities and resources. They aren't blocked and are basically non-traumatic incarnations.
- Karmic healing can do healing on traumas or blockages that you have from past lives. It helps you both in your current life and in other incarnations because your soul isn't necessarily only incarnated in the physical form you have now.
- Since karmic trauma is often very difficult to process, it may be crucial to have a professional karmic healer or regression therapist to support you. You can do karmic self-healing if you are well-grounded in yourself and able to distinguish between past life traumas and the present.

NO MEDITATIONS

I don't have any karmic meditations you can do yourself. This is because it is a more difficult healing method where, as a starting point, there isn't the same "one-to-one assistance" from the lineage as in epigenetic healing. Incarnation relationships and angels often contribute with healing. Karmic healing takes place in a slightly different spiritual dimension than epigenetic healing, which is more closely linked to earthly life and our biological lineage. It is therefore good to have a trained healer who has a good, powerful healing channel and routine in karmic healing work.

CHAPTER 8

HEAL YOURSELF

About how to heal yourself and your life

You have now read about the support there is from the spirit world and the different ways to work with themes, relationships, resources, opportunities, blockages and traumas. I have tried to pass on my methods that I use every day and have seen work so many times, and you have heard stories from my life and some of my course participants' lives where working with the spirit world has made a positive difference. Basically, though, I mostly see myself as a facilitator. The help and support of the spirit world doesn't depend on me or others. It is always there and you can reach out for it yourself. This is important for me to say.

In this chapter, I will give you some tools and healing meditations that you can use to get support in your everyday life or to work specifically with particular relationships or themes, depending on what inspires you. Before you start self-healing, I want to tell you a little bit about what is involved, what normal reactions you can get and what to do if the reactions seem too intense. There is so much good to be had in the self-healing work that I would like to share with you.

WHAT IS SELF-HEALING?
(See illustration "Self-healing")

Self-healing is about reaching out to, and receiving from, the spirit world. You can use self-healing to ask for help for the day or the future, or you can receive healing for the beliefs, blockages or traumas that prevent you from living in harmony with yourself – exactly as if you are receiving healing from a healer. Self-healing meditations are in their essence meditations that bring you into a state where you are able to let your nervous system and sensory apparatus connect with the presence of the spirit world and thereby receive help and support.

When you meditate, it is important that you are in a place where you don't have to relate to the outside world but can come into deep contact with your inner self. You can also listen to music that brings you peace. Pay attention to your calm state of restful, meditative consciousness; once you have found that place, you will be able to get into that state even if there is unrest around you, or you are moving around and more awake. When you have finished meditating, you need to be completely centred in yourself again. You have just had a deep inner or possibly spiritual experience, and you must return to being present in the outer world again. If you don't feel in good contact with your body, or grounded enough, you can imagine that there are thick roots coming out of your feet, which seek to attach themselves to the ground. A good walk, a piece of nice dance music or just looking around and orientating yourself in the room can also give you peace and a feeling of coming back into your body again.

***

Self-Healing Meditations: Structure
Healing meditations always proceed as follows:

- You set an intention for the healing
- You come into an inner meditative peace
- You connect with the pillar of light
- You receive the healing
- You make sure to regain full awareness of the day, a feel for your body and grounding again

> After the intention and connecting with the pillar of light, the meditations can vary depending on which theme or relationships you want to work with (the intention).

***

SET AN INTENTION

In order for you to get something out of the healing, it is crucial that you start by setting an intention. What do you want out of the healing? Do you want support for your day and thereby the feelings, thoughts and physical experiences you will be subjected to during the day? Are there any particular themes such as low self-esteem or performance anxiety that you would like to address? Or are there any relationships that are difficult and for which you would ask for healing? Perhaps you have been in an accident or another physical trauma on which you would like to work – then the self-healing is about a situation. If you set an intention, the direction of the healing becomes more precise, and the spirit world can support you better. Healing is, after all, a collaboration between you and the spirit world, so by setting an intention you express what you want with the contact. If you don't have a specific intention, you can also simply ask for healing for what you need today. The self-healing is for you, for situations you have encountered before or are facing now.

HEALING ON ALL FOUR PLANES
(See illustration "The four planes")

Even if you set an intention, you will always receive healing on several planes. You can ask for healing on an arm that is painful after a fall, but that arm may be associated with some thought patterns that put pressure on you or are otherwise not good for you. Perhaps there is also something emotionally connected to it. So even though you have "only" asked for healing for the pain in your arm, you will find that the spirit world also works with mental and emotional aspects, so that you are healed and released on several levels. This is perfectly normal. As I wrote in the first chapter, we humans consist of four planes, and healing works on all four planes.

Healing will also always support your innermost essence, i.e., what is the kernel in you. So if something is blocking your essence, the healing will work with those blockages. For example, if there is something from your childhood or your lineage that is getting in the way of you being able to live in harmony with yourself, the healing will support it, as I have discussed in the chapters on karmic and epigenetic healing, as well as the one on the inner child. Healing will also support you in your aptitudes. In other words, healing will always support a process that will make you thrive more in your life. Through self-healing, your consciousness comes more in contact with yourself and your soul essence rather than with the patterns you have developed to adapt to the family or society in which you have been living. This leads to you being able to thrive and unfold with the qualities that were previously blocked.

CONNECTING TO THE PILLAR OF LIGHT
(See illustration "The pillar of light")
In the first chapter, I told you about the pillar of light and, when you have to sit with the healing work yourself, it is extra important to focus on the fact that this is a dimension between the physical and the non-physical: a dimension with which your soul is very well acquainted because it has been there before. When we are born, we come down through it. When we die, we are drawn up through it again. The body also knows it because we are in contact with it – when we sleep or meditate, for example. This means it is a completely safe place, which is filled with a loving presence.

When we are doing self-healing, we are training in sensing presence, and the pillar of light is presence. For a start, you must have an intention to contact the dimension between the physical world and the spirit world, i.e. the pillar of light. Allow yourself to imagine that you are surrounded by a loving, safe presence. Perhaps you experience it as a shining presence. Your soul recognises the presence, and your system begins to relax all by itself. You can practise with some of the short meditations on my website, which are free. You can connect with the pillar of light through express-grounding, for example. Everyone can do this; it is a completely natural contact between the individual and the spirit world that exists in all people.

You just have to feel the contact, the presence and the love that is there. Because it is so simple and easy, it would be good to start with practising having that contact before moving on to the more developmental meditations.

GOOD FEELINGS – AND UNPLEASANT ATMOSPHERES

The vast majority, when doing healing meditations, will have a feeling of warmth flowing through their body, a loving, supporting presence and a sense of peace. You may feel happy, grateful and touched. Many will experience getting support, an overview, peace and clarity of thought – many positive things. You may also come into contact with a great deal of exhaustion, either from your current situation or an old exhaustion that you haven't acknowledged. You may have been overly busy and said to yourself that there was no time or possibility of giving in to it right now. Then you have begun to flee from fatigue as a survival mechanism. Maybe you have even dissociated a little from your contact with your body, a bit like a child who refuses to sleep, even though it is totally exhausted, speedy and tense. When that type of exhaustion shows up, give in to it and give space to the healing and rest.

You may also experience a flurry of thoughts; this is perfectly normal. Your brain is used to having first priority, and now you are switching to another state of consciousness that can cause a reaction. I usually describe it in such a way that your thoughts are in a cloud over your head. They may well be there, and the cloud is welcome to blow away while you experience a calmness in you, further down in your body. The image of sitting up against a tree in a quiet area in the countryside on a lovely, peaceful summer day gives an impression of the calm, deeper state of consciousness that can arise. If you are having difficulty keeping your thoughts at a distance, notice if you feel something a little uncomfortable, either in your body or in your feelings, a trauma or an insecure state, and ask for healing for it. The thoughts are a bit like a catapult seat that makes you leap away from what can be "dangerous." When you ask for healing to the place in the body or the feeling that is being revealed – or to the very pattern of fleeing or dissociating – then you will be able to both release this and calm your thoughts. You may also experience reactions that feel uncomfortable. You are working with traumatised stuff, and the healing supports those places in your system where you haven't been able to process anything before. You can get in touch with previous experiences in your life. It may give some of the same reactions as there were at the time they happened. For example, you may access an old anxiety or insecurity. Maybe you do healing on something that happened when you were seven (or thirty) years old. If you are starting to get the same unpleasant atmosphere as you did back then, take a deep breath and try to feel that it isn't about now. Notice that it is old fear, and ask for extra healing to the age you were when this atmosphere arose. Then the part of you that has been tense and pressurised will be able to start relaxing. If necessary, read the chapters on the inner child and the trauma work again if you want to remind yourself how healing of earlier ages can be beneficial for you today. It may also be a good idea to seek professional help. You are feeling the discomfort or coming into contact with the trauma or belief because you are ready to deal with it. Look at it and take responsibility for the state now. But it may well be that it must be addressed in collaboration with a loving, experienced practitioner or therapist and not just through self-healing.

PHYSICAL REACTIONS

Some people also experience physical reactions. For example, the body may react with tingling, dizziness or nausea. The tingling can be due to the body reacting to your contact with something which once frightened you. Your soul has sort of been pushed out of your body, and you may have energetically "pulled your legs up under your body" when it happened. As I wrote earlier in the chapter on trauma, we humans have a link to the animals and their reactions to shock. Their autonomic nervous systems shift from alarm to safe; they flex their muscles, releasing over-energy; and they carry on. If our muscles are tense because we are keeping some emotions or thoughts tightly locked in, we may experience twitching when the trauma is released and the blood flow in the body can improve. You may have had the feeling that you had to wriggle free of something, that you have had to run away, but instead went into a frozen state. Perhaps you feel like kicking out a little, or your arm twitches. This is completely normal, as the body completes the movements it didn't have the possibility of doing in the actual situation. If you feel dizzy or nauseous, let your feet touch the floor, try relaxing your body and ask for healing through grounding. Pay attention once again to what age you were when the fright occurred, or the age from which the overwhelming feeling or situation comes. If you ask for healing specifically for that experience or that age, you will experience a greater connection for a longer time.

Nausea is another reaction that tells you that you have something inside you that isn't good for you and that your body needs to remove it so you can move on with your life. The feelings come out as a kind of poison that is about to leave your body. If you have nausea, try again to notice what the psychological feeling is behind it. For example, if it is insecurity, try asking: How old was I? What experience was it? Ask for healing for it. This part of you has at one point been in an overwhelming situation, and when healing comes to it, there will be space for it again.

Short-term headaches may be a third reaction. When there is more blood flow through your muscles from relaxation, there will be different types of waste products in your body that are released, like lactic acid for example, because there has been a lack of oxygen in your muscles. Always drink plenty of fluids to increase the excretion of waste products and be sure to get plenty of fresh air, which can ease the headache. You may find that you become very hungry and that you need extra vitamins and minerals after these slightly more powerful healings, as the body has used a lot of energy and is building up again after gaining better access to muscles and organs. For although the meditation may only last a quarter of an hour or half an hour, the process can easily continue for days, weeks or months afterwards. Restoring or rebuilding your system is a demanding process and you may experience an increased need for proteins or other nutrients. Follow what feels good for your body.

SEEK HELP IF IT GETS TOO MUCH

Both positive and slightly more unpleasant reactions are completely normal in self-healing. They are part of a process that is good for you on so many levels, where you get to train your spiritual abilities and get in touch with your soul essence and the life you are living today. However, always remember that you have a responsibility for your own processes, so if something is too big for self-healing, you may need to get hold of a healer, a psychologist, an SE therapist or another professional practitioner or therapist. Self-healing can't be done alone if you have very big themes with which to work. However, it can easily support your work with the practitioner or therapist. If you are nervous or are holding back from using self-healing, use a professional instead. Support and security are paramount to working with trauma and major themes.

It is best to start with the easy healing meditations, and notice how you react to self-healing. A strong reaction doesn't have to be a bad sign; it may just mean that you are ready, but it is important that you feel safe with healing and the spirit world before moving on.

***

Exercise: What drains you and what recharges you?
This exercise gives you an overview of what in your life makes the most room for your soul essence to live in harmony with yourself. It is therefore a good one to start with.

Here's how you do it:

- Make a list of which activities in your life drain you and which recharge you. What do you feel happy doing? Having a nice time with a friend, staring into an open fire or going for walks in nature? And what are you good at? Are you good at sewing, baking, driving a car or dealing with children and animals? Now look at the list and think about how much time you spend on each one. We can't only do what recharges us because we also have our chores that we have to complete. But do you spend enough of your precious time on good things? What does it take for you to spend more time on the good stuff? Is there anything that needs to be cleared out, and if so, how can you do it? Which patterns and habits hold you back from doing what is good for you?

- Now make the same overview of your thoughts. What occupies your mind during the course of a day? Do you think bad thoughts about yourself? Are you your own worst critic? What positive beliefs and thoughts do you have about yourself and the world? Why do you think like that, and how can you practise thinking more positively and/or neutrally about yourself? What is the cause of your negative, destructive thought patterns? What do you need to address?

- Now go down to the emotional level and create an overview. Do you have deep, negative feelings about yourself? Do you feel that you aren't worthy of love or that you have to do something to be allowed to be part of the gang? Many negative feelings come from earlier, overwhelming situations – from when you were very little – which won't necessarily be repeated in your adult life. They are like a stone in your shoe and there is no reason to have a stone in your shoe. What good feelings do you have about yourself and life, and in what situations do you have good feelings? What would it take for you to create a better balance in your emotions? What feelings hold you back? Where do they come from? How do you notice how you would like things to be?

- Once you have an overview of the different themes, connect yourself with the pillar of light and ask for healing for the patterns that keep you from thriving in relation to your activities, your thoughts and your feelings.

***

Exercise: Relationships – who is draining you and who is supporting you?

The following exercises will help you become aware of how you feel in different situations and relationships. They don't contain contact with the spirit world but an overview that you can use to target the spiritual work you want to do.

***

WHAT DRAINS YOU ÷	WHAT RECHARGES YOU +

Examples:	Examples:
Shopping	Taking a walk in the woods
Washing up	Enjoying a cup of tea
Too many people around	Chatting with a good friend

Exercise: Family gatherings

Notice how you react when you are going to attend a family reunion. What are your feelings before, when you are there and after? Here you will get a sense of whether there is something that isn't working. Are you nervous and insecure beforehand? Do you lose touch with yourself along the way? Or are you completely drained and uneasy afterwards? If so, relationship work will be an exciting way to get deprogrammed and healed in your relationships. If you are feeling well, strong, warm in the heart and feel received, then use the good experience and atmosphere to support you in other areas of your life where you don't have the same feeling of being received. Then both the bad and good experiences of being at family gatherings can be used to make good headway in your life.

***

Exercise: Negative thoughts about yourself

What ten negative thoughts do you regularly have about yourself? Write them down so you can spot them more easily when they start appearing in the back of your head again.

***

Exercise: Other people's beliefs

Listen to your unconscious, hidden thoughts and beliefs, and try to find out who has instilled them in you. Whose voice is it? And when was it said? When have you sensed those beliefs? Now you know at what age you need to work with yourself and what relationship you should examine so that that relationship has no power over you and your thoughts any more.

***

Exercise: Reprogramming your thoughts

Reprogramming your thoughts: What positive thoughts can you use to promote your self-worth, dynamism and so on? Repeat these thoughts very often every day for an extended period of time.

***

CIRCLE EXERCISES

Person
Bodily reactions
Beliefs/Thoughts
Emotional Reaction

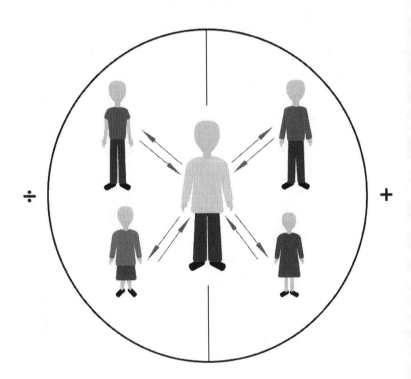

***

Exercise: Overview of your relationships

This exercise allows you to visually spot some patterns that are repeated in your relationships and where the given patterns first appeared. Both the good relationships and the bad relationships are being changed. The same relationship may well be both draining and positive for you. Pay attention to what triggers negative feelings in you and what is good for you.

	NEGATIVE ÷	POSITIVE +
PERSON e.g., brother, mother, friend, boyfriend, girlfriend		
BODILY REACTION e.g., tired, drained / light		
BELIEFS/THOUGHTS e.g., powerless / easy to be myself		
EMOTIONAL REACTION e.g., sad, shrunken / warm, happy		

Once you have an overview of where the bad patterns have started, you can start asking for healing for the younger, tense, limited version of yourself. Some professional help may be needed, but start with the bucket exercise, healing your inner child if it is about childhood or healing past situations if it is about something later in your life.

The good relationships teach you who you are, when you are thriving, when you feel safe and in that state your soul essence and your nervous system will be able to strengthen their collaboration. You will more and more consciously be able to choose better people for yourself and start training to be in a good relationship to yourself. By recognising what you need in a relationship in order to be open and yourself, you can begin to treat yourself more and more in that way.

EXERCISES FOR EVERYDAY LIFE

Collaboration between the spirit world and your daily life is important. If you train yourself to have contact with your soul essence and support from the spirit world in everyday life, you will have trained the contact and trust for when the greater challenges in your life occur. On a daily basis, you will be able to benefit from using contact to your innermost essence, where you are at peace and where you can sense yourself and others. You get the opportunity to be centred in yourself and will be better able to navigate in everyday life without losing your basic sense of self.

In this work, the connection with your soul essence and the pillar of light is crucial. This contact to yourself and the supportive presence you find here gives you an opportunity to come into a peaceful state in a few seconds and connect with your feeling of being centred in yourself again. The connection is a rapid way to down-regulate your nervous system and come down into more of a parasympathetic nervous system response. With this, you will automatically achieve a heightened sense of your body and of being able to stand your ground better. You suddenly have an opportunity to cease reacting on autopilot and catapult seat, which otherwise causes you to lose contact with yourself in certain situations and then go into survival or freeze mode. That is why training this contact is really important, as it provides a good basis for your further collaboration with the spirit world and your own development.

***

Examples of good healing meditations for everyday life are:

- Asking for healing for the day
- Asking for healing to release the day and process the day
- The bucket exercise
- Asking for healing of the past, present or future
- Strengthening your intuition
- Questions for the spirit world
- Contacting your guides
- Contacting your angel team
- Contacting Archangel Gabriel
- Contacting Archangel Raphael
- Contacting Archangel Michael
- Contacting your guardian angel
- Contacting deceased relatives
- The shutting-down exercise.

I go in depth with some of these exercises below.

***

Exercise: Grounding with the pillar of light

You can use this exercise several times a day. It takes less than a minute, but you will notice that it allows you to be relaxed and have more energy in everyday life. You come into immediate contact with a healing presence, and it provides physical, mental and emotional security and relaxation, where you can receive healing and support.

Here's how: Make a habit of making contact every time you wash your hands or something else you do often.

What you get out of the exercise: When you find that you are a little tense or under pressure, you and your system will more and more seek to return to the good state in contact with your essence and the pillar of light.

Eventually you will find that the good state becomes your base and from there you will be able to be more centred in yourself, stronger, more present and more energised.

***

Exercise: The pillar of light as a buffer between you and the pressure from the outside world

Here's how: Notice how you react in a supermarket late in the day. Do you get stressed? Tired? Sad? Or aren't you bothered by all the other people who are there? If you are negatively affected by crowds of people and atmospheres, it would be good for you to train yourself to be surrounded by the pillar of light in that situation so that your nervous system has more sense of its wonderful presence rather than the chaos around you. If it isn't enough to find peace and feel good again, it would be good for you to start training and sensing the contact with your guardian angel or a dear deceased relative in the pillar of light in peace at home. Remember that the pillar of light is not literally a pillar, but a dimension between the physical and the non-physical, which is why you can sense the presence of the guardian angel or the dear deceased relative, who can envelop you with peace, caring and love. You can use that contact to support yourself and your nervous system in the supermarket situation or other potentially overwhelming situations so that you can feel something that is nice and safe instead.

What you get out of the exercise: When you and your sensory system experience security, you get more contact with your body and soul again and you can shut the chaos of the outside world out of your nervous system. Remember that stress and turmoil are passed on through the ability of our sensory apparatuses to perceive our surroundings, so this little self-healing meditation with the pillar of light and guardian angel helps you start to find peace inside. At the same time, you automatically start sending out peace and energy to your surroundings. Instead of being hit by a wave of stress, you send out a peaceful, down-to-earth, loving energy that other people's senses have the opportunity to mirror. This contact with the pillar of light and the spirit world allows you to be increasingly able to control or observe what your senses are preoccupied with perceiving.

***

Exercise: The shutting-down exercise

Many highly sensitive people need to learn how to regulate their senses to a balanced level. This exercise will help you draw in your sensory antennae a little and become rooted in yourself again. You won't be shut off from your feelings for other people, but part of the over-sensing, which is very stressful, will be stopped by you having this focus. Think of it a bit as going from being long-sighted to being near-sighted and having closer contact with yourself than you have with other people. It is a matter of training that requires some self-discipline, but feel how relaxed you are in mind and body after you have done the exercise. Then feel how tense you become with other people when you unknowingly come to "open up for your senses" again, and then train yourself to have the same relaxed feeling when you are with other people. Feel that you are being filled with precisely the amount of loving, warm, caring energy you need. Think of something good and safe. Imagine feeling your own inner white light or inner core (or soul). Let it fill your whole body and a little outside your body too.

Source: *When The Spirits Come Calling*.

N.B. In fact, the shutting-down exercise isn't about you shutting off, but more about sensing where you are in relation to the outside world than about the outside world itself.

***

Exercise: The bucket exercise

This exercise is about letting go of what you have been carrying from other people, or how you have been affected by them; where you have been disturbed by other people's energy, such that you have lost touch with your own energy and attitudes. In the exercise, you release the energy lovingly and constructively; you don't send the bad energy back to the person but get it carried over into the light. You can imagine a dear deceased relative as the person or a guide who takes the bucket away from you and lightens the energy again.

BUCKET EXERCISE

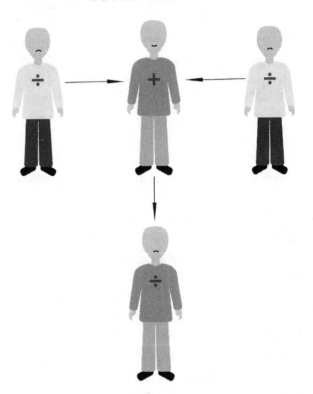

Here's how: Connect with the pillar of light and put your intention on letting go of other people's energies, moods, tensions and blockages. Connect with the things by which you have been affected: for example, another person's anger. Put it in a bucket and let the spirit world carry it over into the light. Ask for healing for yourself so that you can get centred in yourself and possibly become better able to support the other person or stand your ground. Ground yourself again.

What you get out of the exercise: You release the physical energy and emotional patterns that you have absorbed from other people during the day. You are filled up with the energy that is right for you instead.

N.B. You can also do the bucket exercise with a situation that has overwhelmed you or made you sad. This exercise can also be used to release old problems or emotional burdens that you have previously picked up from family, friends or work. Put them in the bucket and let the spirit world carry them over into the light.

***

Exercise: The reverse bucket exercise
(See illustration on taking responsibility)
Just as others put something in you that really belongs to them, you could also put something in others that really belongs to you and that you need to get processed, both so that the others can stand in their light and so you can stand in yours.

Here's how: Connect to the pillar of light. Connect with what you have put out on others, feel that you get it back, and ask for healing for it. Ask for healing so that you don't put negative stuff out on others again or affect them badly in other ways. Remember not to let yourself be overwhelmed by guilt and shame when the bad stuff comes back because now you are taking responsibility, and the spirit world will always support you in that – it will never reject you.

REVERSE BUCKET EXERCISE

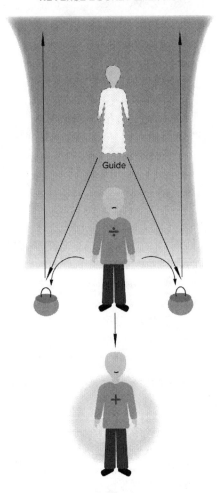

What you get out of the exercise: In the reverse bucket exercise, you get the opportunity to heal and process what others have been carrying around for you when you couldn't take responsibility for it yourself. You can do something actively to bring your energy back to you and wish all the best to those who have been negatively affected by you.[10]

***

Exercise: Training your sensory apparatus

In addition to training the pillar of light and being in the presence of it and the spirit world, there are other ways to train your sensory apparatus in sensing conscious beings and becoming aware of the blind spots in your senses. This exercise is one way. It trains you to sense the presence of consciousness here in the form of your physical helper. However, the spirit world is also consciousness, so you are indirectly training to sense the spirit world. The exercise will also make you aware of where you have reduced sensory ability, trauma and blockages. You can heal these areas or the physical, mental and emotional experiences that emerge, or you can get help at another time.

Here's how: You need two people for this exercise. Sit or stand in the middle and let the other person walk around you. You may have open or closed eyes, possibly with a blindfold. If you do it with open eyes, only look ahead while the person is moving around you. You shouldn't follow the person with your eyes, but sense where he or she is. Say what you experience: "Here I can sense you" and, "Now I can't sense you." When you can't sense the person, he or she may take a few steps back until you again sense the person moving slowly. Since you have a blind spot there, you will possibly get in touch with something that has made you reduce your sensory ability in that place, either because you have retracted your antennae so as not to be harmed, or because part of you is in a frozen state. You may also be over-sensitive right there because your sensory system is over-active.

All you have to do in this case is to make a mental note that you will have to process this later. This is necessary if your sensory system is going to be able to function optimally again.

What you get out of the exercise: With this exercise, you train the senses that have nothing to do with your sight, but are about sensing presence and consciousnesses near you. This is exactly what you need to sense the spirit world. In addition, you can feel where you have the strongest sense of other consciousnesses, for example, by your shoulder, at your back and so on. Those places where you don't feel the presence, there will often be a blockage or a trauma.

TRAINING YOUR SENSORY APPARATUS

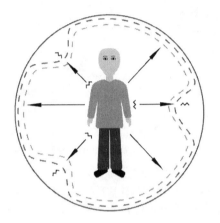

Senses that orientate themselves based on
atmosphere and presence.
Blind spots (your boundaries have been crossed).
The capacity for sensing is smaller.
Pay attention to where you don't sense so well.

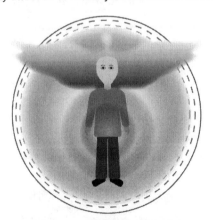

The sensory apparatus is re-established through healing.
Access to our soul essence is stabilised and
the spirit world becomes easier to sense.

TRAINING YOUR SENSORY APPARATUS

Well-functioning sensory apparatus.
You sense equally well all the way around your body.

Sensing in the energy field.
Good sensing in front via eyes and sense of smell.

HEALING MEDITATIONS FOR PERSONAL DEVELOPMENT

These exercises are more demanding, so it is good if you have practised contacting the spirit world first by doing the earlier exercises.

***

Exercise: Physical tension healing meditation

Your body remembers everything you have experienced, from before your birth to the person you are today. You may have repressed some things or carried over experiences from before you acquired language and a more functioning memory and consciousness. These early imprints sit very deep in your nervous system and in your way of reacting. If you have any physical disabilities or tensions, it may be a good idea to take a closer look: 1. What positive and negative effects do they have on you? 2. Can there be mental or emotional blockages coupled with the physical tension?

And in that case: 2a. If there is a mental blockage, when did it arise? What is it about? Where or who did you get it from? 2b. If there is an emotional blockage, what is the atmosphere? Which situation or age did you get it from?

Once you have grasped the cause of the blockage and asked for help with it specifically, you will find that the healing process or the insights come more easily and that more of your energy and your light or your resources are liberated.

For example, if your physical tension is about a feeling of abandonment as a three-year-old, you can heal the three-year-old so that the feeling of abandonment disappears and the feeling of being allowed to be here returns along with a feeling of joy and movement.

Here's how: Connect with the pillar of light and set an intention to heal the physical tension and the beliefs and emotions held in it. Ask for healing of what is hidden from an old physically, mentally or emotionally overwhelming experience so that you can get centred in yourself again. Get grounded.

What you get out of the exercise: This healing meditation is used to do healing on blockages of a physical, mental or emotional nature. It is good for trauma and blockages which are hidden in muscle tension.

HEALING MEDITATIONS FOR YOUR INNER CHILD

These exercises go in and heal at the specific times when a blockage or trauma has arisen, as I discussed in the chapter on the inner child. These meditations can be intense, but also very rewarding.

***

Exercise: Foetal Healing
(See illustration Foetal healing)

As a foetus, you are affected by what you karmically and epigenetically have with you and the mother inside which you are lying and growing, as you have been able to read in the previous chapters. This exercise provides a kind of detox of the energy currents and mental and emotional atmospheres that may have been stressful for you as a foetus. The nervous system and early experiences are healed so that as much as possible of your soul and nervous system can collaborate today.

Here's how: Connect to the pillar of light and ask for healing for your inner foetus. Let the foetus be enveloped by the loving healing presence, which can be, for example, the Archangel Gabriel or the Virgin Mary. Receive the healing. At the end of the meditation, you merge with the little embryo so that you can integrate its original soul essence into your current nervous system and can maintain that state in your current life.

What you get out of the exercise: Your nervous system begins to regenerate based on how it would have been if there hadn't been any blockages, and the collaboration between your body and your soul can therefore work unhindered. It allows you to stand stronger in your life, with a new contact to security, and trust in life being good. Be prepared that there will be some positive fundamental changes in you over a long period of time and that this may require extra fuel. There is simply a physical, mental and emotional growth taking place, just like when the foetus was growing in the womb. Specifically, it may mean that you will need extra protein, minerals and vitamins for a period of time.

***

Exercise: Healing of birth/new-born child

When a person has had a good birth, the little infant acquires trust and self-confidence, the feeling that it can master being physically present. But for many people, it doesn't happen like that. If you have had near-death experiences, your mother has almost died, or you have been anaesthetised during childbirth, you may lose confidence in your own inner strength. Keep in mind that the soul essence during birth is slightly displaced in relation to the survival mode which the body inhabits during birth. If you don't feel safe again after you have been born, you can have your nervous system regulated down into a relaxed state to restore contact to your entire soul essence.

The next step is whether you are well received, by a midwife or parents, or whether there are some states of shock associated with the actual reception. Here too trauma or blockages can occur.

Here's how: Connect with the pillar of light, imagine that a small child – who is you – is on its way out, and give healing to it. This may, for example, be for the times during the birth when a little extra rest may be needed. Childbirth is a slow process and in this meditation you receive healing for that process so that the soul essence and the body have a good collaboration before the birth. There are many from the spirit world who help with this birth process and there are people waiting with love for the arrival of the little infant. When the little infant is ready, it will begin to come out, all by itself, with the pauses and rest periods needed along the way. Pay attention to the feelings and beliefs that emerge, and ask for healing for those which need resolving. When the little infant comes out, pay attention to who receives the little new-born. It could be yourself as an adult. At some point, pick up the little you and pay attention to the contact between you two. Here you will sense your own being completely without the traumas and blockages you get later in life. It is a contact with the purest part of yourself expressed through the small, new-born eyes that look up at you with a completely pure consciousness. There is a loving exchange between the new-born-you and the adult-you – a merging for which there is healing available so that there is space for your soul essence.

What you get out of the exercise: You will be more centred and stronger in your own life when you get healed of the traumas that have taken place at a time for which you have neither language nor memory. You will regain a mastery of being here physically and a merging with both your original vulnerability and the power you have with you in your soul essence: the feeling of succeeding and being received. These are some basic understandings that mean that the adult-you will have a completely different foundation with which to step out into the world.

***

Exercise: Self-healing with your lineage

You don't always have to know that there is a problem with your lineage to use this exercise. Perhaps you have a theme of not succeeding at anything, and because you ask for help with it, you get the help of a deceased person. It could also be that you already know that your theme or your blockages are about something in your lineage. That is the intention you set.

Here's how: Connect to the pillar of light and ask for help with the theme or relationship with which you have challenges. Receive the healing that comes. You can also get reinforcement for things you are already good at as a soul – resources you would like to have strengthened.

What you get out of the exercise: If a problem has arisen earlier in your lineage and been passed on to you epigenetically, it will heal your current life if the deceased, for example, goes in and takes responsibility for patterns that he or she has set in motion.

DREAM WORK

Dreams are important because they can be of great help in your understanding of yourself, your problems and where you stand in your life. There are often solutions to be found in dreams if we look closely, and that is precisely why they can be a good tool to use to move forward.

Dreams can be a mixture of the things that you have experienced during your day, remnants of feelings that you have picked up, or regular stress dreams. And then there are those dreams where the spirit world is teaching us something or where the subconscious is showing us the way forward. Within these, there are definite prediction dreams where you are being prepared for something that is going to happen. These dreams are often clear in such a way that you intuitively know their contents will be actualised. Some people have these dreams often, and others have them only as an awakening to realise that there is more between heaven and Earth. The most common dreams to work with are those that help us process different thoughts, feelings and experiences and teach us something new.

Dreams can work on many levels. Sometimes a single dream can actually contain several interpretations because it can be interpreted from both a mental approach and a spiritual approach. When I work with dreams, I sense whether I should focus on the:

Physical level: Practical; what should I do in the physical world?

Psychological level: What mental problems are being processed? What behaviour does the dream reveal?

Spiritual level of development: There are messages in the dream that represent new knowledge and healing.

In the following, you will get an easy introduction to how you can start working on your dreams from my perspective. You can read about dreams in many places, but this is my way of looking at them.

Dreams often contain symbols such as numbers, figures, stones, nature, fairy tales or people who have a meaning for you. The number 3 can mean many things: for example, the trinity of faith, hope and love or the tarot card no. 3, which is the empress-love-goddess-fertility-growth. Or 3 can be your lucky number. Nature is also often an important element in dreams, so here different animals or flowers can make sense. A sunflower can be your own inner sun or your solar plexus that gets energy. When you dream of different people, think about what those people mean to you. Where in your life do their qualities matter to you right now? Is it someone you don't like, or is it someone you look up to? And why are they popping up right now? Sometimes deceased people come to tell you something, and it is precisely in these dreams that it is especially important to remember to interpret on a spiritual level, as this interpretation often hold the possibility of liberation and growth on deep levels.

Like symbols, colours are a very powerful element in dreams. If you dream of a particular colour, you may be lacking in that colour. For example, dreaming of red may mean that you lack drive or bodily awareness or currently don't have the feeling of being able to find your roots. As with the other symbols, colours can have many meanings, so your sense of exactly where you yourself have a problem is important. You can continue working on the colour of which you have been dreaming either by becoming aware of the problem the dream was about or by visualising the colour throughout your body or in the chakra that it stimulates.

When working with dreams, be curious and analytical. What can the dream mean to you? Use your intuition to find the answer. Always remember to sense if the interpretation makes sense to you. If it doesn't, try again until you have the feeling that something resonates inside you.

***

Exercise: Dream chart

Use the chart below to note down the symbols, people, and colours you dream of. It will be able to help you understand your own "language" with the spirit world.

	TRADITIONAL INTERPRETATION	YOUR OWN INTERPRETATION
PERSON		
CHARACTER		
ATMOSPHERE		
SYMBOL		
COLOUR		
ANIMAL		

- Fill out a chart with the symbols you dream of because then you will find it easier to interpret your own dreams.
- Fill out a chart with the people you most often dream of so you become aware of the qualities and aspects of yourself that you are working on right now.
- Fill out a chart of the colours of the seven chakras, heat, cold, joy, and so on, and sense what you yourself understand by working with them. If there are several colours that come to mind and feel important to you, describe them as well. New colours and shades of colours that come in your dreams later or have already been there are also important to include.

ANGELS AND GUIDES

Even if you carry out self-healing alone, you are never alone. You have a network of guides, angels and the dead who are always ready to help you. The different angels have different qualities and are therefore good at different things. In general, it is the case that:

- The Archangel Gabriel represents recharging and caring. It often heals the most hurt and neglected places through an infinitely loving presence. Gabriel is a good heart recharger for caregivers.
- The Archangel Raphael stands for calm, inner peace and acceptance of yourself and your situation. He especially helps with accepting difficult feelings and creates hope, harmony and peace in body and mind.
- The Archangel Michael stands for strength, inner strength, clarity and drive. You can call on him in particular when you need protection – for yourself, your children, your home or something else. His energy is good at helping you get rid of bad patterns and habits and stay strongly centred in yourself.

It may therefore be beneficial to ask for help specifically from one of these angels if you know that you need healing in a particular area. If you want to get in touch with the angels, connect with the pillar of light, find peace, and ask for contact with a particular archangel or your guardian angel in order to get to know their presence and energy. There will be quite a lot of healing for you in the presence of the angels. When you have practised a bit more, you can connect with the pillar of light, and then precisely those angels will come who can best help you. You can read much more about the angels and their specific qualities in my other book, *When The Spirits Come Calling*.

YOUR SOUL, YOUR LIFE

We are now coming to the end. I hope I have managed to inspire you to both seek within yourself and reach out for help in the spirit world. It is very important for me that we each live our precious lives now in accordance with who we are – our soul essence – because when we do that, our souls radiate out into the world, spreading good energy like ripples in the water. We get a better life for ourselves and create better lives around us, ultimately helping to heal all of humanity.

In this book, I have given you some tools that I use myself and that I have seen many people use with great results during the twenty years I have worked with the spirit world. However, the help isn't dependent on me or other spiritual professionals; it is always there.

***

Your soul is eternal. You have lived before and you will live again. I hope you find your path.

***

Endnote

10 The reverse bucket exercise is inspired a lot by the Ho'óponopono Hawaiians' way of healing conflicts. Taking responsibility on a very deep level with an honest and loving approach to oneself and to those one has influenced, and letting the healing happen. It is about forgiveness, healing and harmony. If you want to read more about Ho'óponopono, I can recommend the book *Zero Limits*, mentioned in the bibliography.

**AT MARZCIA.DK YOU CAN
FIND THESE MEDITATIONS:**

Guardian angel express grounding

Pillar of light

Control of your sensory system

Bucket exercise

Reverse bucket exercise

Epigenetic lineage of mother and father

AUTHOR BIOGRAPHY

Marzcia Techau (born 1971) is a Master of Science in Biology, Speaker, Author, Spiritual teacher, Clairvoyant Counsellor, Healer, Reiki Master and Somatic Experience Practitioner working with Peter Levine's Somatic Experience Method®. For the past 20 years, Marzcia has worked with a blend of scientific and spiritual understandings of life. A part of her master thesis was a healing study of plants at the University of Copenhagen. Later she worked as a research assistant at a study of energy healing effects on cancer survivors at the University of Southern Denmark.

She has worked as a medium and have been taking clients for 22 years. The recent years she has worked as a teacher of healing and clairvoyance, as a writer and been giving talks to a broad audience. In her teachings, her talks as well as in her books she emphasises the relationship between natural sciences and the spiritual world by applying new knowledge and scientific research in her dissemination of healing, human development, and spiritual practice.

She has previously written the book "Når ånderne banker på" ("When The Spirits Come Calling" – not available in English) and participated in several TV shows, podcasts, interviews, etc., including "The spirits return" on TV3+, "Healing the last resort" on TV2 and recently "My sister sees ghosts" on DR (2022–23).

PREVIOUS TITLES BY THE AUTHOR

Techau, Marzcia og Karen Seneca. *Når ånderne banker på: Mit liv blandt engle og ånder.* Copenhagen: Rosinante 2013. (Not available in English).

NOTE TO READER

"In this book, I have given you some tools that I use myself and that I have seen many people use with great results during the twenty years I have worked with the spirit world. However, the help isn't dependent on me or other spiritual professionals; it is always there. Your soul is eternal. You have lived before and you will live again. I hope you find your path."

MS in Biology, Author and Spiritual Teacher, Marzcia Techau

***

The intent of the author is only to offer information of a general nature to help you in your quest for emotional and spiritual wellbeing. In the event you use any of the information in this book for yourself, the author and the publisher assume no responsibility for your reactions.

The exercises and work described in the book can largely be done on your own. As always when we work with ourselves, both physical and mental reactions can occur. If you are in any doubt about whether it is good for you to perform the exercises yourself, or if you have big themes to work with, I will always advise you to make contact with a healer, a psychologist, a Somatic Experiencing therapist or another type of professional practitioner or therapist.

www.marzcia.dk www.facebook.com/marzciashealingscenter

REFERENCES

Alexander, Eben. *Proof of Heaven: A Neurosurgeon's Journey into the Afterlife*. New York: Simon & Schuster, 2012.

Archive for Research in Archetypal Symbolism. *The Book of Symbols*. Cologne: TASCHEN, 2010.

Aron, Elaine N. *The Highly Sensitive Person: How to Thrive When The World Overwhelms You*. New York: Birch Lane Press, 1996.

Bernstein, Albert J. *Emotional Vampires: Dealing with People Who Drain You Dry*. New York: McGraw Hill, 2012.

Bruce-Mitford, Miranda. *Signs and Symbols – An Illustrated Guide to Their Origins and Meanings*. London: Dorling Kindersley Ltd., 2019.

Byrne, Lorna. *Angels in my hair. The True Story of a Modern Irish Mystic*. New York: Harmony Books, 2011.

Chopra, Deepak et al. *The Shadow Effect. Illuminating the Hidden Power of Your True Self*. New York: Harper Collins, 2010.

Goleman, Daniel. *Social Intelligence. The New Science of Human Relationships*. New York: Bantam Books, 2006.

Golodnoff, Ulrik. *Crowley Tarot ABC*. Sphinx, 2009. (Not available in English).

Hay, Louise. *Heal Your Body*. Carlsbad: Hay House Inc., 1984.

Hart, Susan. "Spejlneuroner, kontakt og omsorg." *Psykolog Nyt*, nr. 11, 2007. (Not available in English)

Levine, Peter A. *Waking The Tiger: Healing trauma*. Berkeley: North Atlantic Books, 1997.

Levine, Peter A. *In an Unspoken Voice: How the Body Releases Trauma and Restores Goodness*. Berkeley: North Atlantic Books, 2010.

Lipton, Bruce. *The Biology of Belief: Unleashing the Power of Consciousness, Matter and Miracles*. Carlsbad: Hay House, 2006.

Myss, Caroline. *Anatomy of the Spirit: The Seven Stages of Power and Healing.* New York: Harmony, 1996.

Newton, Michael. *Journey of Souls: Case Studies of Life Between Lives.* Woodbury: Llewellyn Publications, 1994.

Newton, Michael. *Memories of the Afterlife: Life Between Lives – Stories of Personal Transformation.* Edited by Michael Newton, Woodbury: Llewellyn Publications, 2009.

O'Malley, Mary. *The Gift of Our Compulsions: A Revolutionary Approach to Self-Acceptance and Healing.* Novato: New World Library, 2004.

Palsteen, Lotte. *Din teenager er dit spejl – tør du kigge i det?* Grønningen: Grønningen 1, 2020. (Not available in English).

Redfield, James. *The Celestine Prophecy: An adventure.* New York: Hachette Book Group, 1993.

Vitale, Joe. *Zero Limits: The Secret Hawaiian System for Wealth, Health, Peace, and More.* Hoboken: John Wiley & Sons, 2007.

Stefansson, Finn. *Symbolleksikon (The Encyclopaedia of Symbols).* Copenhagen: Gyldendal 2009. (Not available in English).

Techau, Marzcia og Karen Seneca. *Når ånderne banker på: My life among angels and spirits.* Copenhagen: Rosinante, 2013. (Not available in English).

Virtue, Doreen. *Archangels and Ascended Masters: A Guide to Working and Healing with Divinities and Deities.* Carlsbad: Hay House, 2004.

Wilson, James L. *Adrenal Fatigue: The 21st Century Stress Syndrome.* Smart Publications, 2001.

O-BOOKS

SPIRITUALITY

O is a symbol of the world, of oneness and unity; this eye
represents knowledge and insight. We publish titles on general
spirituality and living a spiritual life. We aim to inform and
help you on your own journey in this life.
If you have enjoyed this book, why not tell other readers
by posting a review on your preferred book site?

Recent bestsellers from O-Books are:

Heart of Tantric Sex
Diana Richardson
Revealing Eastern secrets of deep love and
intimacy to Western couples.
Paperback: 978-1-90381-637-0 ebook: 978-1-84694-637-0

Crystal Prescriptions
The A-Z guide to over 1,200 symptoms and their healing crystals
Judy Hall
The first in the popular series of eight books, this handy
little guide is packed as tight as a pill bottle with
crystal remedies for ailments.
Paperback: 978-1-90504-740-6 ebook: 978-1-84694-629-5

Shine On

David Ditchfield and J S Jones

What if the after effects of a near-death experience were undeniable? What if a person could suddenly produce high-quality paintings of the afterlife, or if they acquired the ability to compose classical symphonies? Meet: David Ditchfield.

Paperback: 978-1-78904-365-5 ebook: 978-1-78904-366-2

The Way of Reiki

The Inner Teachings of Mikao Usui

Frans Stiene

The roadmap for deepening your understanding of the system of Reiki and rediscovering your True Self.

Paperback: 978-1-78535-665-0 ebook: 978-1-78535-744-2

You Are Not Your Thoughts

Frances Trussell

The journey to a mindful way of being, for those who want to truly know the power of mindfulness.

Paperback: 978-1-78535-816-6 ebook: 978-1-78535-817-3

The Mysteries of the Twelfth Astrological House

Fallen Angels

Carmen Turner-Schott, MSW, LISW

Everyone wants to know more about the most misunderstood house in astrology — the twelfth astrological house.

Paperback: 978-1-78099-343-0 ebook: 978-1-78099-344-7

WhatsApps from Heaven
Louise Hamlin
An account of a bereavement and the extraordinary
signs — including WhatsApps — that a retired
law lecturer received from her deceased husband.
Paperback: 978-1-78904-947-3 ebook: 978-1-78904-948-0

The Holistic Guide to Your Health
& Wellbeing Today
Oliver Rolfe
A holistic guide to improving your complete health,
both inside and out.
Paperback: 978-1-78535-392-5 ebook: 978-1-78535-393-2

Cool Sex
Diana Richardson and Wendy Doeleman
For deeply satisfying sex, the real secret is to reduce the heat,
to cool down. Discover the empowerment and fulfilment
of sex with loving mindfulness.
Paperback: 978-1-78904-351-8 ebook: 978-1-78904-352-5

Creating Real Happiness A to Z
Stephani Grace
Creating Real Happiness A to Z will help you understand
the truth that you are not your ego
(conditioned self).
Paperback: 978-1-78904-951-0 ebook: 978-1-78904-952-7

A Colourful Dose of Optimism
Jules Standish
It's time for us to look on the bright side, by boosting
our mood and lifting our spirit, both in
our interiors, as well as in our closet.
Paperback: 978-1-78904-927-5 ebook: 978-1-78904-928-2

Readers of ebooks can buy or view any of these bestsellers by
clicking on the live link in the title. Most titles are published
in paperback and as an ebook. Paperbacks are available in
traditional bookshops. Both print and ebook formats are
available online.

Find more titles and sign up to our readers' newsletter at
www.o-books.com

Follow O-Books on Facebook at **O-Books**

For video content, author interviews and more, please subscribe to our YouTube channel:

O-BOOKS Presents

Follow us on social media for book news, promotions and more:

Facebook: O-Books

Instagram: @o_books_mbs

X: @obooks

Tik Tok: @ObooksMBS

www.o-books.com